Managing People

Jane Weightman BA, MSc, PhD is a psychologist and an honorary lecturer in the Manchester School of Management at UMIST. Since joining in 1980, she has carried out research into a wide range of management-related topics. Previously, she worked in the field of mental handicap as a researcher, teacher, lecturer and county advisor. She has written widely in a range of journals and her books include *Competencies in Action* (1994), also published by the CIPD.

Other titles in the series:

Core Personnel and Development
Mick Marchington and Adrian Wilkinson

Employee Development
2nd edition
Rosemary Harrison

Employee Relations
2nd edition
John Gennard and Graham Judge

Employee Resourcing
Stephen Taylor

Employee Reward
2nd edition
Michael Armstrong

Managing Activities
Michael Armstrong

Managing Financial Information
David Davies

Managing in a Business Context
David Farnham

Managing Information and Statistics
Roland and Frances Bee

Personnel Practice
2nd edition
Malcolm Martin and Tricia Jackson

The Chartered Institute of Personnel and Development is the leading publisher of books and reports for personnel and training professionals, students, and all those concerned with the effective management and development of people at work. For full details of all our titles please contact the Publishing Department:

tel. 020-8263 3387

fax 020-8263 3850

e-mail publish@cipd.co.uk

The catalogue of all CIPD titles can be viewed on the CIPD website:

www.cipd.co.uk/publications

PEOPLE AND ORGANISATIONS

Managing People

JANE WEIGHTMAN

Chartered Institute of Personnel and Development

© Jane Weightman 1999

First published in 1999

Reprinted 1999, 2001

Design by Curve

Typeset by Paperweight

Printed in Great Britain by
The Cromwell Press, Wiltshire

British Library Cataloguing in Publication Data
A catalogue record for this book is available from the
British Library

ISBN 0-85292-784-3

The views expressed in this book are the author's own and
may not necessarily reflect those of the CIPD.

Chartered Institute of Personnel and Development, CIPD House,
Camp Road, London SW19 4UX
Tel.: 020 8971 9000 Fax: 020 8263 3333
E-mail: cipd@cipd.co.uk Website: www.cipd.co.uk
Incorporated by Royal Charter. Registered charity no. 1079797

Contents

PREFACE   vi
FOREWORD   vii

PART 1 THE FUNDAMENTAL CHARACTERISTICS OF PEOPLE   1
    1 Introduction to managing people   1
    2 Individual differences   15
    3 Learning   35

PART 2 THE CHANGING WORLD OF WORK   53
    4 Factors influencing work, jobs and employment opportunities   53
    5 Differing work patterns   64
    6 The management of work-related stress   80

PART 3 OPTIMISING THE PEOPLE CONTRIBUTION   97
    7 The move from compliance to commitment   97
    8 Finding and selecting people   111
    9 Nurturing people   126
    10 Leadership   140
    11 Influence and persuasion   154
    12 Motivation   168
    13 Stimulating improved performance   184
    14 Performance management   197

REFERENCES   213
PROFESSIONAL STANDARDS INDEX   222
INDEX   223

Preface

This book is written to the CIPD core management standards for managing people. Part 1 looks at ways of understanding individual people. Part 2 examines the environmental factors that affect the work of individuals. Part 3 contains practical material on how to manage people more effectively. Each of the following chapters starts with a small case study based on a true situation to emphasise the issues dealt with in the chapter. At the end of each chapter I ask you to consider how you would react to the case study in the light of what you have read and give my views. Each chapter also contains, from time to time, questions to ask yourself, set in a box. These aim to give you the opportunity to reflect on what you are reading and to apply it to your own situation. I hope you will use some of them. It is only by trying to apply the material to real situations that you will learn to manage people more effectively.

Foreword

Welcome to this series of texts, which are designed to complement the Core Management syllabus. The role of the personnel and development practitioner has become an important part of the total management of all types of organisation in the private, public and voluntary sectors. A fundamental element of this role is the ability to comprehend and contribute to the overall goals, performance and outcomes of organisations. This is the purpose of the Core Management syllabus: to equip personnel and development practitioners to understand and appreciate complex business and managerial issues, and to develop their skills so that they can play a full role in that process.

Jane Weightman's book examines the role of managing people whatever the organisational setting of the business. It stresses the fundamental requirement to understand the nature of individual characteristics and differences and the extent to which work, as a shaping and defining activity, has undergone profound change. A major issue, for all managers, is that of maximising the contribution of employees within the organisation. This book demonstrates that all managers who have any kind of responsibility for managing the employment relationship need to have a sound understanding of this management process, regardless of their specialist responsibilities and whether or not they are in a line or functional role.

Professor Ian J Beardwell
Head, Department of HRM
Leicester Business School
De Montfort University
Leicester

Part 1
THE FUNDAMENTAL CHARACTERISTICS OF PEOPLE

1 Introduction to managing people

OBJECTIVES

By the time you have read this chapter you should be able to:

- understand the different systems of thought involved in analysing how to manage people such as the social sciences and personnel management

- be aware of some of the central debates in this area such as unitarist versus pluralist, management versus leadership and the ethics of leadership.

Managing people is an extremely important part of making organisations work well. Managing people means acknowledging that the people in the organisation are the most important part of getting things done. The human resources approach assumes that no amount of clever work with figures, or of expenditure on the latest technical equipment, will deliver anything unless people agree to work in co-ordination with each other. This applies to everyone in the organisation. An alternative view is that of industrial relations writers, who assume there is basic conflict in the employment relationship. This makes mutual accommodation necessary because the conflicting interests can never be reconciled. Whichever perspective you hold, studying the management of people will be useful to you at work. By understanding other people and how they interact you will be able to get things done more easily. Managing people means understanding both formal and informal relations between people at work.

WHAT ARE THE DIFFERENT STRANDS OF THOUGHT THAT INFORM THIS AREA?

Ideas and evidence from several traditions are used by people trying to understand the issues associated with managing people. First, there is material that originates in the social sciences: psychology, sociology, political theory and philosophy. These subject areas have developed individual specialisms in organisation analysis and practical management applications. Second, there is material from what Americans call 'management specialists': ideas, research and practice that are devoid of any academic pedigree but look particularly at work organisation from the management perspective. This group includes work by various sorts of experts. It may be that of successful managers who have written autobiographies – for example Sir John Harvey-Jones (1994), one-time chairman of ICI, or Bill Gates (1996), founder of Microsoft. It can be that of systematic researchers of management such as the study of core competencies in organisations by Prahalad and Hamel (1990). Or it can be management textbooks where assumptions are made about the nature of the management task, for example Handy (1985). Subsections of this body of material contain contributions from people working with a personnel, training and development perspective, nowadays often called 'human resource management'. Each of these specialisms has a contribution to make to understanding managing people.

Gareth Morgan's highly influential academic book *Images of Organization* argues that there are seven quite distinct ways of looking at organisations (see Table 1). Each is a different sort of probe into a complex area, and each is appropriate for giving us an insight into some aspect of an organisation's working. An

Table 1 Ways of looking at organisations

---

1 Organisations as machines
  With orderly relationships
    clearly defined parts
    determined order

2 Organisations as organisms
  With adaptation to the environment
    life cycles
    dealing with survival

3 Organisations as cultures
  With patterns of belief
    daily rituals
    own language

4 Organisations as political systems
  With authority
    power
    right to manage or individual rights

5 Organisations as brains
  With think tanks
    strategy formulation
    corporate planning teams

6 Organisations as psychic prisons
  With trap of one way of thinking

7 Organisations as instruments of domination
  With some having influence over others
    work hazards

Adapted from Morgan (1986)

organisation is all of these things at the same time. Only by having a variety of strategies for investigating or 'reading' the situation can we be effective. At the very least, if we fail we can try something else.

This book tries to use material from a wide range of different disciplines. The first part concentrates on the individual and contains material from a psychological perspective – with its language of behaviours, motivation and feedback. Part Two mostly uses the language of social science to look at the variety of work situations and emphasises such things as context, cultures, norms and roles. Part Three looks at the organisation as a whole and uses language from a variety of disciplines: from engineering comes the language of systems, structures and control; from politics the language of power, influence and authority; from management that of overall responsibility; and from theology the language of vision, leadership and commitment. As you may begin to understand, the study of managing people involves the range of human language and analysis. It is always the case that there are several different ways of looking at the same behaviour or issue. Sometimes these differing views are compatible – but not always. Learning to deal with this diversity of views is at the heart of managing people.

What are the social sciences?
The two disciplines in social science that are most relevant to managing people are psychology and sociology. Other disciplines normally included among the social sciences are economics, geography and political theory. They are not included in detail in this book, although the idea of people as economically and politically active is important for understanding organisational life and is included in discussions about the analysis of how things are done throughout the book.

When I tell people that I am a psychologist they usually say something like 'Oh, I'd better be careful then, as you can read my mind.' Fortunately for us all, this is not true. I cannot read people's minds. Another confusion is that psychology is the same as psychiatry. It is not. Psychiatry is concerned with particular accounts and treatments of people with mental illness. So what is psychology?

Psychology is normally defined as the study of behaviour. It may be animal or human behaviour. Such a study can include detailed descriptions of particular behaviours – for example how we learn; it may also include some analysis to try to account for why these behaviours happen in the particular way they do. By looking at the underlying structures and hypothesising about the effects of previous experience and the environment in which it takes place we try to understand questions such as:

- Why do people choose to do different things?

- Why does one person reject this course of action when the previous person did not?

- Why do decisions change?

Psychology usually tries to account for the behaviour of individuals, but it includes what happens to them when they are in groups large and small.

A particular branch of psychology relevant to our needs is organisational psychology. People working in this area apply the findings and models of psychology generally to work organisations. They also carry out research into organisations to try to improve our understanding of them. As with all psychology, there is particular emphasis on the effect on individuals and their effect on others. This includes questions such as: What do managers do? How do groups influence each other? How can changes in people's behaviour be dealt with most effectively? I use several examples from this discipline in this book.

Sociology is concerned with the social, group and institutional aspects of human society. There is some overlap with all the other social sciences. What distinguishes sociology is a desire to understand the influences and agreed norms of the institutions of society that affect the behaviour of its members. Sociologists look for generic (general across groups) concepts and patterns that can help to explain social activities. They examine such questions as: what are the roles we play? Which institutions are most dominant in society? Does the nature of the community affect the individual's choice of career? How do bureaucracies work? What distinguishes professionally qualified workers from other groups? Are there different sorts of conflict? What are the effects of different cultures?

These enquiries can then be used to analyse specific examples such as the role of a senior manager, the profession of accounting or the culture of the National Health Service. Of all the social scientists, sociologists are the most interdisciplinary – sharing insights and ideas with economists, geographers, psychologists and political scientists as well as with philosophical and religious writers. This interdisciplinary tradition is useful for analysing and understanding work organisations. This is particularly so when we try to understand a specific organisation as compared with another or the position of a particular group within the organisation.

Other disciplines from social science that are also involved in studying organisations and the people in them are economics when considering performance management – see Chapters 13 and 14; and political science when considering power – see Chapter 7. Some other disciplines are also influential: for example, history and cultural studies will tell us about the context of organisational behaviour while engineering provides some of the control and systems language that certain management writers use.

Social scientists use many different methods to study behaviour. Some psychologists use biological methods to study the biological basis of behaviour. This sort of study seeks to determine what the limits of behaviour are and what the inherited components of behaviour are. For example, how is memory stored in the brain (see Greenfield, 1997)? Other psychologists use a scientific framework but study behaviour. They set up carefully controlled experiments in the laboratory where everything is kept the same except one thing; any differences in behaviour are then accounted for by the variation in the one factor. As an example of this type, one study tells us that any sort of additional attention to people at work improves their productivity on routine tasks – the so-called 'Hawthorne effect' which was found in some early work in factories by psychologists (Mayo 1939).

Yet other psychologists and sociologists study behaviour in its natural setting, trying to use systematic description and analysis to account for the behaviour. This might involve questionnaires, interviews or observation. Examples would be studies of stress in teachers or of how new recruits behave on an induction programme. Sociologists use interviews and observation to collect their data. Sometimes they use outsider, non-participant, observation; on other occasions the study is conducted by a member as participant observation. Unlike psychologists they rarely use controlled experiments, preferring to study real situations.

You will notice that throughout this book I refer you to some quite old writings. The development of any discipline is never even; sometimes there is a rapid increase in knowledge and theory while at other times progress is slower. The last decade or two has seen a marked change in confidence in psychology and sociology, with an increase in the variety of views. In psychology there are two areas in which there has been marked consensus about genuine development: physiological psychology, where study of the brain's mechanisms are increasing our understanding; and developmental psychology, with its analysis of how children develop. In other areas there is rather less sign of new fundamentally agreed theories. Writers have indulged in introspection and self-analysis (see, for example, Kline 1989) probably because the basic description and analysis of behaviour have been done and psychology and sociology are now looking at higher-order models and integrations. Many are looking to applied areas such as the study of the mentally ill or of work organisations to help develop these higher-order models using the basic research of older references as their starting points.

Can I think of any behaviour at work that a psychologist could usefully study and why such a study could be useful?

What contribution to understanding my situation at work could a sociologist make?

What is personnel management?
Personnel work is directed at the employees – finding them, training them, arranging for them to be paid, explaining management's expectations of them and justifying management's actions to them. The personnel function of management is carried out by all managers. In all but the smallest organisation it is also partly carried out by specialists. This is to ensure consistency of treatment and to operate systems such as performance appraisal and job evaluation, which only have value on an organisation wide basis. Personnel specialists are concerned with satisfying employees' work needs and with modifying management policy and actions that might otherwise provoke an unwelcome reaction. Human resource management (HRM), a more recent term for

specialists, implies a more strategic view of the part people play in the success of an organisation. It might be said that HRM is when the chief executive uses personnel.

Personnel management is defined by Tyson (1987) as managing the employment relationship. Tyson suggests that this has led to three types of personnel department. First is the clerk of works type, where the department gives administrative support but has no involvement in business planning; the principal activities for personnel staff are recruitment, record keeping and welfare. The second type is like the contracts manager, concerned to meet each event with a system as part of the policy network; personnel staff are involved with informal agreements and understandings and so become part of the political life of the organisation. The third type is that of the architect, who seeks to build up the organisation as a whole; personnel staff devise explicit policies which affect the corporate plan, and have a system of controls integrated between line management and personnel. Not surprisingly, professional personnel managers prefer to see themselves as architects. For example, HRM experts claim expertise in managing change – a crucial area for most organisations.

As a line manager your relationship with the personnel function will depend upon its role in the organisation. If it is 'clerk of work' it will be a source of information and support for quite specific things. If it is 'contracts manager' or 'architect' you are more likely to be discussing, debating and deciding with its members how to proceed in particular areas.

Personnel management professionals are currently inclined to call themselves human resource managers which emphasises the strategic business orientation. Useful books in this area are by Marchington and Wilkinson (1996) and Foot and Hook (1996).

Do we have a personnel department? What sort is it? When did you last use it?

Unitarist or pluralist?
Many would like to think that the history of thought on organisations is developing in an evolutionary manner. This has

the attraction of integrating everything currently known, implying that the latest is the best. This is certainly the position of many management consultants who peddle their versions of the latest thinking to various organisations. However, there seem to be fundamental differences in the basic assumptions of some schools of thought that have not been reconciled or integrated. This has been well described in a technical book by Burrell and Morgan (1979), who argue that some contrasting assumptions could never be reconciled. For instance, some people believe that organisations can be one happy family, believing in the same ideals as a strong leader; technically this is called the 'unitarist view' and an example might be the Body Shop and Anita Roddick. Other people believe that organisations are made up of people with a variety of views and beliefs that should all be heard; technically this is the 'pluralist view' and most universitites are examples. The choice between unitarist and pluralist views seems to be a matter of personal preference – see, for example, our choice of leadership model discussed in Chapter 10.

For those of us concerned with the practical business of managing people in organisations as part of our working life, it is perhaps best to be pragmatic – to try to find the analysis that seems to make most sense of the particular problem presented at any one time rather than hold to one view through thick and thin. This approach of 'it depends on the situation' is called contingency theory.

> Do you prefer the one-happy-family approach of the unitarist or the diversity of the pluralist?

Managing or leading people?

Whether we hold a unitarist or pluralist view when it comes to managing people there are both 'hard' and 'soft' approaches. The hard mechanistic approaches of control management can be compared to the soft concerns of the human relations models of leadership. These are no longer seen as stark alternatives but rather as options that most effective operators will combine in practice. Let us look at some of the practical implications of this in the ways managers behave towards others.

Hard management

The hard approach includes the view that by carefully analysing the work to be done managers can specify exactly how things should be done and so become more efficient. This mechanistic approach has always had the appeal that if we only spend just a little more time and effort analysing things we will have a perfect system. Modern examples of this approach are to be found in some exponents of the quality movement and competencies approach:

- The quality movement is enshrined in two standards – one British, BS5750; and one international, ISO 9000. For example, very detailed BS5750 or ISO9000 quality standards specify the exact nature of the memos that should be sent if there is a complaint.

- The competency movement is an approach to recruiting, developing and rewarding staff that looks in detail at what they should do to meet the required performance. Similarly, competency lists have been seen to include such minute detail as 'smile at the client when they first come to the reception desk'.

An example of this hard approach in catering is the desire to break down the whole job of catering into its component parts and get less skilled, and less well paid, people to do the more menial tasks. This approach expects people to comply with the carefully laid down analysis of what is required.

These hard approaches, where tasks are carefully specified, are useful where a high degree of conformity is required, where there are many temporary or unskilled staff or where there are major crises to be dealt with. Their disadvantage is that the more prescriptive an approach the more people will work to rule and show no initiative as it is 'more than my job's worth'.

Soft management

In contrast, the soft approach to management tends to put the emphasis on getting the right things for people to do. It includes an appreciation of individual styles and motivations. Here there is a great deal of discussion of empowering people to control their own work and of allowing people to express their views on how things could be done better. The softer approach emphasises the fulfilment of individual talents. It is about developing people over a period of time and allowing them to make different contributions at different times in their careers. Some of these softer approaches emphasise individualism and others the building of teams. But all encourage individuals to feel that what they are doing is worthwhile and worth making a commitment to. Some of this is expressed in very caring terms, which makes those from the hard approach suspicious. An example is how some restaurants allow individuals to express their personal service to the customers in a variety of different ways.

These softer approaches emphasise autonomy and collegiality and are most appropriate where the full commitment of the people in the team is necessary – for instance, when a situation is new and everyone needs to deliver a service. An example is when health visitors in clinics were faced with a new recommendation on the best way to put babies in their beds to prevent cot deaths, but no one knew quite which was the most effective way of communicating this to parents. Each health visitor was encouraged to use his or her own personal skills and judgement on how to get the message over to parents.

There does seem to be some need for bringing both hard and soft approaches together. One possible way of doing this might be to systematise some of these softer approaches so they can be evaluated alongside traditional harder methods. One such way was some work I did with my colleague Royston Flude at Kellogg's plc. As our starting point we used a list of competencies issued by the Management Charter Initiative (MCI), the National Vocational Qualification (NVQ) body for management competency standards. We (Weightman and Flude 1996, unpublished) felt that the different competencies could fall into four distinct groups:

- managing activities which were about getting things done and the actions required by the business

- managing the analysis of information and resources to solve problems and reach decisions which involved thinking

- managing people and dealing with one's own and other people's feelings

- managing the vision, values and assumptions that underpin the organisation. This involves understanding one's own values and expressing them in strategic ways.

The first two groups of competencies might be described as the hard approaches to getting the right things done and the latter two groups as the softer approaches. We found that teams needed all four groups of competencies and that the more senior managers were, the more of the second two groups of competencies they needed and the less they could do of the first, although they often still had to supervise competencies from the first two groups. The exercise highlighted the need for different competencies within a team and the fact that both hard and soft competencies are required for sustainable, excellent performance. This work was based upon the Motivational Driver Model (or FIN) developed by Royston Flude.

The importance of trying to develop both hard and soft competencies can be seen within almost any organisation. There are times when we need the analytical, hard competencies of making the most of the resources available to us. At other times we have to deal with other people and our own feelings using the softer competencies. It may be that we personally take more easily to one group of competencies or the other. If we are to become useful members of a work organisation we do need to try to acquire at least a modicum across the whole range.

The move from the hard approaches associated with management to the softer approaches that are associated with leadership is at the heart of much discussion in personnel and management circles. See for example the change of vocabulary in the syllabus for CIPD core management from the previous set; now there is great emphasis on the soft skills of leadership and developing commitment. This is reflected in the changes in the content of this book compared with its predecessor (Weightman, 1993).

Can you think of three hard approaches used in your organisation?
Can you think of three soft approaches used in your organisation?
What are the effects of these? Are they appropriate?

The ethics of leadership

If we are going to manage other people what are the ethical issues of doing so? Ethics have become a popular topic in many business schools. This sounds great but as Rowe (1997) points out, ethics can be taught in two very different ways. It can be taught using the models of absolute values, or as theologians and philosophers call them 'first principles' – that is, the absolute right and wrong ways of doing things. But it can also be taught in terms of how we all have our own way of seeing things. In this view values are relative to individuals and the situations in which they find themselves – the right way depends on the context. The first is very much like the unitarist view of organisation and the latter like the pluralist view.

The first model of the leader having the right way is always popular with senior people as it leads to an elite of people who have some claim to a special connection to absolute values. The special claim might be based on ownership, ability, personal charm, success or other factors. The second model is more democratic: it argues that we all start from our own unique perspective and we have to prove by argument that our perspective is a better approximation of reality than anyone else's. Users of the first model can claim infallibility whilst those of the second persuasion always have an element of doubt. The first demand compliance, the second rely on credibility to get things done – see Chapter 11 for further discussion.

The ethics of leadership can be seen from each of these perspectives. Is the leader claiming some superior position or does he or she take the democratic approach in order to encourage each person to offer their best? Where you stand on this dichotomy will tell you what sort of leader you are and will also tell you how vulnerable you are to a fall. The absolute version is always less flexible than the contingent model. Chapter 10 deals specifically with leadership but several times throughout the book there will be suggestions on how to influence those who work for you. When you use these suggestions try asking yourself whether some claim for absolute values is appropriate or whether a more democratic approach might be effective. The style of your leadership has implications for you as well as for those you try to lead. I believe that if you try to achieve an unobtainable absolute you are more likely to be frustrated than if you adopt the more pragmatic contingent view of leadership – but then I was ever the pluralist and relativist. Make your own view, but try to know yourself; whichever ethical position you hold, knowing yourself will help you to lead and manage people more effectively.

Chapter 13 has further discussion on the ethics of management, this time on the ethics of managing performance.

FURTHER READING

Foot and Hook (1996) and Marchington and Wilkinson (1996) are excellent textbooks in personnel/HRM. Marchington and Wilkinson is the more serious academic text.

2 Individual differences

OBJECTIVES

By the time you have finished reading this chapter you should be able to:

- understand and explain the principal ways in which human beings differ and the causes of these differences

- understand and explain some of the ways these differences may create problems for the organisation and how this may be dealt with.

NICK'S DILEMMA

Nick was head of a large business team. He was also a very keen sportsman. The team included 20 people based in the office and 20 sales people located throughout the country. The company was celebrating the 50th anniversary of its foundation. Nick was allocated £50 per person to hold some sort of jamboree for his team. The only rules were that there should be some event to which the entire team was invited. How was Nick to decide on what would suit everyone?

Should he capitalise on the cohesive, young group in the office and have some energetic day out such as go-karting? Should he ask for suggestions? Should he arrange a traditional dinner, so no one would be offended? Should he try to emphasise the team or do something more dramatic than the other teams? Would it matter if everyone came, as long as they were invited?

If we are going to work successfully with a range of people we have to come to terms with the fact that there is quite a wide variety of people doing the same job. If we were all the same it would be not only very boring, but also detrimental to the organisation as there would not be a sufficient breadth of experience and opinion when we needed to solve problems. By understanding and tolerating these differences we are more likely to get a co-operative, productive effort from those we come into contact with. This does not mean we have to understand and tolerate all behaviour, indeed that would amount to indifference. So we need to try to influence some people to behave differently, but show some tolerance of individual differences as it is essential if we are to work with other people.

I have included here three concepts about individual differences to demonstrate how we can analyse the differences between people. Having analysed and understood the differences we might then want to change that person's behaviour at work. By understanding why an individual may behave differently we are more likely to be able to accept the difference or to find a convincing way of helping him or her to change rather than just saying 'I want you different.' The three concepts used are personality, perception and diversity.

WHY PEOPLE HAVE DIFFERENT PERSONALITIES

We all need to understand other people so we can make friends, understand our families and influence each other. An important step in our understanding is the need to see things from the other's point of view, an extremely difficult thing to do. To do this we have to analyse something about his or her personality. One way of doing this is to have some models to help us analyse. In other words, one way of understanding more about the nature of individual differences is to look at the theory of personality.

In everyday use, the term personality describes the impression a particular person makes upon others. It is the differences in our personalities that sum up the difference between you and me. Inevitably there are lots of theories of how and why our personalities are formed and what they are derived from. There is no one best theory of personality. The theory or theories that seem to account best for our own and other's behaviour will vary from time to time and place to place. We are likely to be attracted to theories of personality that fit our own personality. Our view of personality will also affect how we interact with people. It is well worth understanding what that view is so we can interpret the effect we may have on others and modify it where appropriate.

Some models for understanding individual differences of personality are given here, but there are many others. Three main contrasting schools of thought on personality are those of the psychoanalysts, the behaviourists and the humanistic psychologists. These three views are still the most influential. Let us look at each in turn and see what insights they can offer on behaviour in organisations.

> Can you think of three very different personalities at work? What does each of them do that is particularly useful at work?

Psychoanalysis

The psychoanalysts are dominated by the theories of Sigmund Freud (1962), developed from his work in Vienna at the beginning of the twentieth century. Freud concluded that personality consisted of three separate parts. The 'ego' is made up of the individual drives that focus a person's nature. It will make people act differently from those around them and interpret the world differently. The 'superego' is learned from society. It represents the injunctions of parents, schoolteachers and other important members of society about what is acceptable behaviour and what is not. The superego can have a modifying effect on the ego, which suggests that basic drives are modified by society. The 'id' consists of the basic, animal instincts that make us get going and become involved with our surroundings.

Freud argues that personality develops through a series of traumatic stages when these three aspects of personality are in conflict, and trying to get them into some sort of harmony is the business of maturing. The classic stages described by Freud include the following:

- First, the early period of breast feeding with its implicit intimacy between mother and child which leads to anguish when the child is asked to give it up.

- Second, the anger felt by children over the external control implicit in toilet training.

- Third, the disapproval demonstrated by society of childhood sexuality.

- Fourth, the difficulties for all of us in learning to control anger and aggression in socially acceptable ways.

Freud argues that these traumas get pushed to the back of the mind but continue to affect our behaviour into adulthood. The most obvious example is what we call the Freudian slip, when we say something with a hidden meaning instead of what we intended, for example, if an individual uses a favourite brother's name when talking to the less preferred brother. Another example is that the early experience of toilet training may result in a need for order and tidiness in adult life.

As well as the general implications of analysing how we deal with anger and aggression, another way in which a Freudian approach can be useful at work is his idea of defence mechanisms. These are devices we subconsciously use to defend ourselves from being psychologically undermined. We use these when we feel under stress and they give us relief. The most common defence mechanisms are:

- Fixation: individuals become rigid and inflexible and stick to known procedure and behaviours.

- Rationalising things: individuals cover up their behaviour and contributions with elaborate explanations.

- Regression: individuals behave in a less mature or childish way than is usual or appropriate.

- Projection: individuals attribute their own motives and feelings to others where this is inappropriate.

Perhaps Freud's greatest contribution to our understanding of behaviour in organisations is the message that we must consider the whole person and everything that has happened to him or her to understand his or her personality. The main criticisms of his theories are that they are based on a very small sample of Viennese bourgeois life in the early part of the twentieth century and that by placing so much emphasis on childhood they make it difficult to see what we can do to change ourselves once we grow up. By their nature, the theories are very difficult to test and collect data about.

As an example of how psychoanalytical theory could be used in understanding organisations, Dickson (1976) used a Freudian analysis to look at the work of people in the army. He demonstrated how military life attracts those who like regimentation and orderliness, and suggested that this was due to the individuals' early childhood experiences. With so many people in the military falling into this category there are not enough who can be flexible when the rules, regulations and procedures do not cover a particular circumstance. Dickson maintained that since those with potty training traumas tended to be drawn to military organisations there should be nothing surprising in the fact of military incompetence.

Hans Eysenck was a British psychologist who did much to popularise the subject through books such as *Know your own IQ* (Eysenck, 1962). He was also responsible for the widespread use of the terms introverted and extroverted, originally proposed by the Swiss psychiatrist Carl Jung. Eysenck's main suggestion is that we differ in our basic state of arousal, that is how much stimulation we require to get going. Those with an introverted personality are naturally highly aroused so any extra stimulation sends them into a state of anxiety. By contrast extroverted people are in a low state of arousal and consequently need a lot of stimulation to get them going. This distinction suggests that introverted people will seek out quiet whereas extroverts will thrive in large noisy gatherings. Eysenck (1976) has proposed that there is a continuum from the most introverted to the most extroverted. He has also suggested that people differ on a dimension he calls neuroticism as opposed to stability. Eysenck argues that a stable extrovert has quite a different personality from a neurotic introvert. The logical conclusion from this is that the two individuals' behaviour at work will be quite different; the former could tolerate a more robust environment than the latter, whilst an environment that suited the neurotic introvert would probably seem boring to the stable extrovert. Eysenck did a good deal of research to support his theory but he has been criticised both for the nature of some of the research and for his emphasis on the role of nature and genetics.

Much of our everyday understanding of personality has come from Freud and other psychoanalysts. The usefulness of psychoanalytic models for analysing people at work lies in their message that there may be deep-seated reasons for strange behaviour. The models are also useful in giving us some basic vocabulary to describe the differences between people. However, the drawback of using only a psychoanalytical view of personality is that there is such an emphasis on the early years, and this gives the impression that nothing can be done later about people's personality. It can lead to a feeling of hopelessness if someone does not fit in.

Behaviourism
The behaviourists are dominated by the work of the American psychologist B F Skinner. His main point was that we learn through our experiences and that these experiences affect who and what we become. With others (1953), he explored in minute detail how behaviour is learned – see Chapter 3 for further details. Skinner emphasised the external control of behaviour: we behave in the way we do because of our history of reinforcement or rewards. According to behaviourists, a stimulus evokes a response from the individual, which in turn evokes a reaction that may or may not be reinforcing to the individual. Where the response leads to a reinforcing reaction the individual is more likely to respond in that way in the future. For example, if every time we offer to wash up we are given a grateful hug we are more likely to offer again in the future, assuming we like hugs from that person; if we are told we are washing up in the wrong way, at the wrong time, we are unlikely to offer again, unless of course we like being told off!

By studying observable behaviour and the effect of different rewards given at different times, the behaviourists have built up a detailed technology for specific learning. It has proved highly successful in teaching new skills. Many computer programs for teaching are based on this 'programmed' learning. The idea is to make the instructions as clear as possible and when the correct response is elicited a reward is given: it may well be 'well done' or something more concrete. The behaviourists have suggested that if we can discover which reward, or reinforcement, each individual prefers, learning will take place more effectively.

Reward is defined as that which the person will work for. The process of manipulating people's behaviour by adjusting the instructions, task and reward is called 'behaviour modification'.

There are clear implications here for managing people. If personality is learned and dependent on the history of reinforcement, then managers can institute a suitable system of rewards to elicit the behaviours that are required to run an organisation effectively. The only task is to analyse the desired behaviours and reinforcements in sufficient detail and with enough accuracy for individuals to be motivated to behave appropriately. Luthans and Kreitner (1975), amongst others, develop this idea. They give reinforcement schedules, analysis of behaviour and the training necessary to enable managers to put it into effect. The application of their ideas does seem to improve productivity and can be seen in such training schedules as that of the McDonald's fast food chain.

The limitation on applying this approach comprehensively is the difficulty of including the idea of intrinsic rewards emphasised by Maslow, as I discuss in Chapter 12. The behaviourist approach also suggests that workers are entirely dependent on managers getting the analysis right, whereas many people work in environments in which some degree of self control and personal responsibility is necessary. There are also ethical issues related to the degree of control and obedience we are prepared to accept at work. Very few of us have difficulty in accepting the use of behaviour modification techniques to teach mentally handicapped children to feed themselves. But most of us would object to having the same techniques applied to us by a manager with complete control over us at work – assuming of course that someone was clever enough to analyse both the task and the rewards accurately enough to persuade us to comply.

Humanistic psychology
Humanistic psychology has been very influential among organisational psychologists and in the study of organisational behaviour. Unlike the other two schools of thought outlined above, it is not dominated by one outstanding figure for it is really about ideals. It is more a description of what 'could' and 'should' be than an analysis of what 'is'. The central belief is that

we all have within ourselves the capacity to develop in a healthy and creative way. The emphasis is on becoming independent, mature adults who can take responsibility for our own actions. There may be distortions due to the vagaries of parents, schools or society but we can overcome these difficulties if we are prepared to take responsibility for ourselves.

Maslow is usually seen as the founding father of this school with his idea of the self-actualising personality (see Chapter 12). He outlined the concept of people who work for themselves to see how far their abilities will take them. By putting this concept at the top of his hierarchy of needs, Maslow was obviously advocating it as an ideal that we should aim for.

Carl Rogers (1967) has also been very influential. He described a sequence of stages that an individual goes through in becoming a fully functional person.

- First is the need to be open to experience and to move away from defensiveness.

- Second is a desire to live each moment more fully and immediately, rather than to relate everything to the past.

- Third individuals increasingly trust themselves physically, emotionally and mentally.

- Fourthly and ideally, individuals take responsibility for themselves and their actions.

As a help in going through these stages, Rogers advocated using other people as a resource to interact with. Only by sharing experiences and developing trust do we come to know and trust ourselves.

Consultants working in organisations will often be operating from this particular standpoint. The enthusiasm for participation in decision making, ownership of ideas, autonomous work groups and developing potential all fit within humanistic psychology. One particular application is the concept of stress and the analysis of sources of stress. The cure is dependent on this diagnosis but usually some increase in openness and trust is advocated with higher degrees of autonomy and self management being associated with a healthier organisation.

The problem with using humanistic psychology is that not everyone shares the ideals. Given the unproven nature of some of the basic tenets, it can be difficult to persuade non-believers of the benefits of the proposed changes.

Can you think of three awkward people at work? Would any of the above theories suggest why they are awkward? If so, how would you approach them differently?

Other theories of personality

One group of theories that has been widely used by people studying organisational behaviour rejects the idea of motivation and single stages in personality development and emphasises the individual's conceptualisation of his or her world. Kelly (1955) introduced the idea that we all construct our own worlds. We each see things differently and interpret things differently using our own dimensions and models; this means we each construe the world differently. One dimension he used was the process of 'attribution', by which we make sense of our world by making assumptions, or attributions, of what is causing things to happen. By having these attributions we hope to be able to predict and control social events. Each of us will have different attributions and so perceive the world differently. By enacting many roles and engaging in continuous change we have constantly to practise this process of construction. Kelly's theory is called 'personal construct theory'. Various devices based on Kelly's original device the 'repertory grid' have been developed to discover what 'constructs' each of us is most likely to use.

A related group of concepts are the social learning theories. These deal with the learning of behaviour and particularly the learning of maladaptive behaviours – see, for example, Bandura (1977). They emphasise dysfunctional – that is, unhelpful – expectancies or self concepts. Expectancies can be dysfunctional in a variety of ways. If we wrongly expect a painful outcome we are likely to avoid a situation. If this is a wrong expectation we may miss out on the good times. For example, if you fear that closeness will bring pain you are likely to act in a hostile way that leads to rejection by others, which in turn confirms the expectation that closeness will bring pain. Dysfunctional self-evaluation can be exemplified in the person who has no standards of self reward and so is bored and dependent on external pleasures. It can also be seen in the person who has set overly severe standards for him or herself, standards which lead to self-punishment and depression. All these can be a problem at work. The recommended therapy from this point of view is modelling, guided participation and desensitisation.

Various models of personality are used in organisations for assessing the personalities of people wanting to join the organisation. Psychometric tests – that is, systematic tests – have an increasing popularity in the assessment of personality. In psychology circles there is much debate about this as the reliability of the tests and the ethics of assessing something as personal and private as one's personality are not clear cut. On the other hand the personality of a candidate is inevitably assessed at interview with a view to seeing whether the candidate will fit in with the work group. Might it not as well be done by a systematic test as by guesswork? A widely used test is the Occupational Personality Questionnaire (OPQ) developed by the British consultancy company Saville and Holdsworth. The various forms have 30 scales of personality attribute covering such things as persuasive, active, modest and critical. An individual profile of these attributes can then be compared with the desired qualities of the person-specification for a particular job. These questionnaires have to be administered by specially licensed people. The results are often then used by others responsible for the decision.

PERCEPTION

Another useful concept in trying to understand individual differences is what psychologists call perception. Perception is the term used to describe the process of selecting, organising and interpreting incoming stimuli. We all do it differently and so perceive a different real world. The real world is so stable and familiar to us it seems curious to discuss the way we perceive the world. But this familiarity and stability of the world has more to do with our own mental processes than the actual sensory input, which is constantly changing. Because we organise the incoming message into our stable view of the world we make it seem stable to us. But your stable world is a different one from mine.

There are several reasons why people may perceive the same situation differently:

- *Physical sensitivity*: human organs are only sensitive to a limited range of things. For example, none of us can see x-rays. Some people are more or less sensitive than others – for example, partial sight or hearing makes a difference to the stimulus received.

- *Selective attention*: we notice some things and not others. For example, at a party we can concentrate on one conversation and ignore others; we focus on what is important to us. If, however, someone mentions our name we usually hear it – even in a conversation we are not part of.

- *Categorisation*: we categorise the cues as they come in. The incoming stimuli are fitted into one of our existing categories – such as concepts, ideas and associations built up in our memory as a result of experience. This process may well be influenced by language; we fit things into our existing pattern of understanding.

- *Limits on our capacity*: we can only deal with a limited amount at any one time. The limit is set not just by how much is coming in but also by the ease of categorising the stimuli. The time we feel most overwhelmed at work is when many difficult communications are coming to us; the office party, when there are probably just as many communications, is nothing like as daunting because the communications are easier to categorise and it is easier to decide what action to take.

- *The environment*: our expectations and the context will determine the kinds of categorisation we will apply. If we are expecting to see our colleague at the airport, it is surprising how often we misidentify someone else before we meet the right person. Whereas if we meet the same person in the supermarket it may take us a little while to remember his or her name.

- *Individuality*: our attitudes and personalities will influence what we perceive. They generate expectations. A prejudiced person sees the behaviour of those they are prejudiced against in a negative way whatever actually happens: a friendly act will be seen as false, a casual attitude as sloppy, a remote stance as difficult – and so on. This in turn will affect the behaviour of the perceiver, creating the beginnings of a vicious circle.

The act of perceiving is a constructive process in which we try to make sense of our environment by attempting to fit it to our experience. The real world is different for each of us as we perceive it differently. As you work with people you will undoubtedly be faced by people perceiving things differently from yourself. Sometimes this will be because of a different job perspective and access to information, sometimes because of the amount of time and commitment we have given the topic. It is usually possible to resolve the difference by means of a discussion that unravels the basis of the different perceptions.

DIVERSITY

So far this chapter has dealt with the psychological models that can help us analyse individual differences. There is also a social component to why people are different. Individuals' cultural and economic backgrounds will influence the norms that are set for them, the socialisation they experience and the choices available to them. Norms are the socially acceptable, 'normal' way of doing things. Socialisation is the process by which our behaviour is shaped by those around us so we fit in and become socially acceptable. Different ethnicity, gender and abilities will also account for individual differences, because individuals will have been treated differently as children and as adults in both overt and covert ways. To say that people are different does not mean that some are superior, merely that their experiences differ.

One aspect of managing people that has attracted attention over the years is how to ensure fair treatment for different people. This has also included legislation on equal opportunities and discrimination about gender and race. Table 2 gives a list of the legislation that to some extent protects people from discrimination. This is known as equal opportunities legislation.

Table 2 **Equal opportunities legislation**

Sex discrimination
Sex Discrimination Acts 1975 and 1986
Employment Protection Act 1978
Equal Pay Act 1970
Employment Rights Act 1996

Racial equality
Race Relations Act 1976

Disabled people
Disability Discrimination Act 1995

Part-timers
European Court of Justice rulings

Ex-offenders
Rehabilitation of Offenders Act 1974

Northern Ireland
Fair Employment (Northern Ireland) Act 1989

The inequality of opportunity that is experienced in selection, training and promotion by women, ethnic minorities and those with disabilities has been hotly debated since the 1960s and is further discussed in Chapter 8.

In many management books, and particularly in personnel or human resource management ones, there is increasing use of the term 'managing diversity'. This is used where in the past a phrase derived from 'equal opportunity' was used. There is a different emphasis as well as a change of vocabulary. The concern of the earlier equal opportunities movements and legislation was to help different groups cope with a dominant male, white, able-bodied culture. Managing diversity is more about valuing the differences people have and using and celebrating these differences. This might include such diversity over:

• qualifications

• accent

• sexual orientation

- caring responsibilities

- learning difficulties

- political affiliation

- spent convictions

- trade union membership

- gender

- ethnic origin

- age.

As the CIPD (1998) points out, the reasons that diversity matters in organisations are:

- It can open up new opportunities through broadening the customer base.

- It is part of the increasingly important ethical stand of organisations.

- It ensures the selection, training and retention of people from the entire labour market rather than part of it only, so the organisation can attract the best talent.

- People want to work for fair employers.

- Organisations are required to abide by equal opportunities legislation.

- Benchmarking against other organisations will show that diversity and equal opportunities are increasingly included in such things as contracts to supply.

For many well established organisations this is still a novelty and far from achieved. For newer, small organisations, particularly in the so called 'gorgeous' industries of fashion, hospitality and performance, there are more examples of the celebration of diversity.

Although it makes rational sense to recruit and develop staff on the basis of their ability to do the job, the judgement is easily influenced by beliefs that are not relevant. Even those committed to recruiting and developing on ability can be prejudiced in ways they do not realise. To give some of the arguments that challenge stereotypical thinking in this area (see IPD 1998):

- *Ability/disability*: performance at school is more related to the socio-economic status of the parent than to ethnic origin. Girls do better than boys. Most disabilities have no practical implications for job performance and more people acquire disabilities as they age than are born with them. We have to be very careful of 'mind sets' that lead us to make unfair assumptions about others.

- *Culture*: the ethnic minority of Great Britain is about 5.5 per cent of the population, and lives mostly in London, the West Midlands and Greater Manchester. These groups have a higher proportion of young people than the white population and tend to live in larger households. In some parts of the country a significant part of the local workforce will be from these groups, in others a rare employee. The important issue is that each individual is recruited and developed for his or her individual capacity to contribute.

- *Gender*: women make up over 40 per cent of the workforce, of whom 44 per cent are part-time. Men are increasingly also working part-time. Two and a half million men and three and a half million women have caring responsibilities for elderly dependants. Approximately 10 per cent of lone parents are men. Caring responsibilities make it difficult to work conventional hours but flexible working can suit a wide range of people who would willingly contribute their best if they could.

Perhaps the important thing to remember in all this discussion of diversity is that focusing on differences tends to group people together and assume there is something wrong. Only by concentrating on the individual and the similarities of what they can contribute can we genuinely use the talents of everyone living and wanting to work in the United Kingdom. In organisations with a performance-management approach to individual staff, managing diversity is less difficult to achieve than those organisations that are set in their ways. Kandola and Fullerton (1998) researched about 500 organisations and reported that old-style, group-based equal opportunities can be developed through strategies that focus on individual performance to manage a wide variety of people with different attributes, concerns, values and needs to achieve the organisation's goals.

OVERCOMING STEREOTYPING AND PREJUDICE

In trying to understand other people we all instinctively use a short-cut method known as stereotyping. This is an essential aspect of dealing with others but can also be a strait-jacket if we do not use it carefully. If you have lost your way in a strange place and decide to ask someone for directions, you do not stop the first person you see; you pick out someone from the surrounding crowd who looks a potential source of good information. You probably pick on someone who is not in a hurry, neither too young nor too old, appearing intelligent and sympathetic. You have a working stereotype of who would be an appropriate person to ask. At work we carry round a series of stereotypes that influence all our dealings with other people.

There is seldom time in working situations to abandon all stereotyping. As a way of approaching matters, especially in emergencies, some sort of working hypothesis is needed immediately. The danger of stereotyping is, of course, that people are not treated as individuals but as categories. This is unreasonable and can be unlawful. It also limits the ability of the person who is overdependent on stereotypes to work with others to the full extent of his or her abilities. A special form of this is the 'halo effect' – some aspect of behaviour overrides behaviour elsewhere; for example, the assistant who is always on time but does poor work is seen as an admirable member of staff. Stereotyping often occurs between departments in organisations. For example, the research staff are seen as earnest, harassed and socially ill at ease, whereas the sales assistants are seen as fun-loving and lively.

Prejudice occurs when stereotyping is taken to an extreme form where we categorise whole groups of people and see them as conforming to prejudged behaviours. Some of these prejudices can be illegal and are certainly inappropriate in the workplace.

Changing our stereotypes and prejudices is not easy. Changing other peoples' stereotypes and prejudices is even more difficult, but we need to try where these are inappropriate. Bringing things out into the open is certainly a help. The PC or 'politically correct' movement, despite some of its absurdities, has been helpful in allowing us to do this. The usual advice for improving our ability to perceive others accurately and therefore with less prejudice is:

- The better we know ourselves the easier it is to see others accurately. Many of the transactional analysis and assertion workshops are about 'knowing oneself'. Intimate discussion and feedback sessions can be useful; indeed the best appraisal interviews could include this sort of feedback – see Chapter 14.

- One's own character affects what one sees in others. Using material in the earlier part of the chapter to see how individual differences arise might help us to deal with this.

- The accuracy of our perceptions depends on our sensitivity to the differences between people. Trying to develop a sensitivity about people that looks below superficial differences is the beginning of wisdom and credibility in managing people.

> When you are feeling aggrieved by the way you have been treated what do you feel has been misunderstood? How could you do something about this? Do you have pet sayings about some of your colleagues? How do you see other departments in the same institution?

Can people's attitude at work be changed?

We have looked at three concepts for analysing individual differences. These might mean they look at work in different ways. If people have different attitudes to work how important is this? What do we mean by attitude? Can those attitudes be changed? The most widely quoted definition of attitude in psychology is that of Allport (1954, p45):

> A mental and neural state of readiness, organized through experience, exerting a directive or dynamic influence upon the individual's response to all objects and situations with which it is related.

Similar is that of Krech and Crutchfield (1948, p173):

> An attitude can be defined as an enduring organisation of motivational, emotional, perceptual and cognitive processes with respect to some aspect of the individual's world.

These two classic definitions state or imply that attitudes have the following characteristics:

- They are related to an object – some aspect of the individual's world.

- They are part of the general way the individual experiences and reacts to this world.

- They are relatively enduring.

- They imply evaluation and feeling.

Katz and Kahn (1978) suggest that attitudes and motivation are intertwined. Depending on the person's motives an attitude can provide the following:

- *Knowledge*: attitudes give a base or framework for classifying and interpreting new information.

- *Expression*: attitudes enable us to indicate what our values are, what self-concept we have and which group values we have adopted.

- *Instrumental*: depending on our past experiences of rewards and negative experiences, we will hold different attitudes to people and experiences.

- *Ego-defensive*: we may hold attitudes to protect ourselves from an undesirable truth or reality.

Most social scientists agree that attitudes are a complex, multidimensional concept that have an emotional and a cognitive aspect to them. For this reason, attitudes can be difficult to change. Some of the techniques that are used to try to change attitudes are:

- The rational approach: as we experience and assimilate material in accordance with our expectations, attitudes and motivation, it is not surprising that a straightforward, rational approach which merely presents the good reasons for why we should change our attitudes and beliefs rarely has much success.

- Social influence: social pressure is likely to have more influence but only where the communicator has credibility and seems an attractive model.

- Emotional approach: emotionally toned communications tend to be more influential than straightforward, rational explanations – as long as the emotion is appropriate and does not raise feeling to a level of anxiety.

Those of us managing people at work and having to deal with a problem over attitude to work might need to examine the problem more clearly. What is the problem? Is the individual's performance poor? Is it affecting others – or is it just a matter of style? Chapter 14 has a section on managing poor performance.

This chapter has briefly looked at models and concepts for analysing individual differences. Part 3 continues this by looking at ways of managing individuals so they contribute effectively.

AND FINALLY...

What would you recommend Nick did about the jamboree? Now you have looked at some of the tools to analyse individual differences would your advice be any different?

I would suggest that Nick try to find a venue that would include as many people as possible but which could also deal with a wide diversity of tastes and personalities. It may be that a day out in work time to some country estate where the active can participate in competitive activities and the gentle can stroll around the gardens is most inclusive. Having some team event during the day for speeches and jokes emphasising 'us' would be ideal. If he imposes his own taste for extreme sports many may feel excluded.

What happened in reality was that the office group decided they should hire a coach and leave after lunch one day for a night out in Blackpool! Many of the sales people and older members of the team did not go.

FURTHER READING

Any good introduction to psychology will have chapters on personality, perception and individual differences. For example:

Hayes N (1994) *Foundations of Psychology*. London, Nelson.

She is a well-established author of introductory books on psychology. I find her very readable and sensible.

Hardy M *and* Heyes S (1994) Beginning Psychology. 4th ed. Oxford, Oxford University Press.

A widely available, simple introductory book written by the pioneers of A-level psychology.

3 Learning

OBJECTIVE

By the time you have finished reading this chapter you should be able to understand the learning process for both individuals and organisations.

LAURA'S LOCAL DIFFICULTY

Laura is the assistant manager of a busy clothes shop. The shop is not part of any chain but owned by its manager who comes into the shop most days but leaves the day-to-day running to Laura. There are five other members of staff on varying contracts and hours. There is no time in the week that everyone is due in. The owner and Laura take pride in knowing their clientele so well that customers can phone up and ask for particular kinds of clothes and the shop will send a suitable selection to them. How can they encourage this expertise in their staff?

How do people learn the names and tastes of customers? How do they remember them? Is it easier to systematise this or to rely on individuals doing it in their own way? Are some sorts of learning about customers easier than others? Are there some sorts of customers who relate better to some staff than others? Should the individual differences between the staff be acknowledged? Does everyone learn in the same way?

At work we all have to learn specific skills to deal with our jobs. We also have to learn to adapt to changing circumstances. If there is one common issue that people at work have to deal with it is change. Where change is involved, so is learning. It may be a new skill we have to acquire, such as a new telephone system or process. We may have to get to know new people whose company has been amalgamated with ours. Perhaps we have to learn the details of the new organisation structure so that we can follow the correct procedure for informing people about a forthcoming meeting. Whatever changes are occuring, they require us to learn something. Chapter 9 deals with the way organisations formally and systematically try to encourage particular sorts of learning to increase the performance of individuals and groups within the organisation. This chapter deals with how people learn. The central importance of understanding learning for managers is that we want people to change some aspect of their behaviour at work, and that inevitably means learning the new way.

Another important aspect of learning in organisations is the form of accumulated learning called experience. It is a crucial part of authority, expertise and effective work. It is seen in the gradual learning of better ways of getting things done that someone who has been in the job some time takes for granted, and incidentally is often overlooked when jobs are being reorganised. A more formal sort of learning in organisations is when people systematically set out to learn a different way of doing something by going on a course or to a conference. A further way of learning is the process of being coached by someone else to improve already competent behaviour such as chairing meetings. All these examples of learning involve a change in knowledge, skills or attitude. Change in behaviour can come about through formal training which is dealt with in Chapter 9, or by more informal processes. Most learning in organisations, and elsewhere, takes place informally and is the subject of this chapter.

HOW PEOPLE LEARN

As well as the purely academic pleasure of trying to understand how people function there are many practical reasons for trying to understand how people learn. Before we can start learning systematically or helping someone else to learn we need to know how people learn. It might enable us to reduce the time it takes us to learn something. When difficulties arise we can start analysing where the problem lies and so do something about it. If organisations are to compete in an ever-changing world they need to assist people to learn the new ways so that they can retain their jobs and contribute to the new processes. Similarly, individuals need to understand how they learn best so they can adapt to a variety of environments and people. So what models about learning are there? It will come as no surprise that there are several different models of how people learn.

Behaviourist theory

Behaviourists are interested in studying observable, measurable behaviour and many of their studies have been of how learning occurs. The two classic studies are those of Pavlov and Skinner.

The Russian physiologist Ivan Pavlov (1927) demonstrated how reflexes could be trained to a new stimulus. He found he could get dogs to salivate when a bell was rung if the ringing of the bell was associated with a plate of food. The dogs learned that the bell meant food and so became 'conditioned' to salivate. Anyone who has had a cat will recognise the pattern – my cats would come whenever they heard a tin being opened or the fridge door opened! This association of S(timulus) and R(esponse) is called 'classical conditioning', or S-R learning. The responses fade if the connection is not maintained. We probably have various physiological responses – for example, raised blood pressure – to specific situations such as a visit to the dentist. These are classical conditioning.

Skinner's (1965) model was more complex. He experimented with rewards and punishment and their effects on animal learning. For example, by rewarding pigeons with corn when they showed suitable behaviour he was able to teach them to play ping-pong. He showed that a response would be learned when it was rewarded, or technically 'reinforced'. This is called 'operant conditioning'. He found that learning took place more quickly by using rewards for positive behaviours rather than by punishing inappropriate behaviours. His maxim is that for effective learning to take place you need a regime of 80 per cent rewards. How many of us manage that at work?

This behaviourist, or behaviour modification, approach has led to many examples of programmed learning such as using praise to reinforce people's good working habits and the use of computer-assisted learning. The important concept to remember about behaviour modification is that learning only takes place if the individual is prepared to work for the reward offered. This model is now felt to be too simplistic for the complexities of applied social systems such as organisations but it is worth remembering as it emphasises the importance of feedback or knowledge of results without which learning is unlikely to be effective.

Experimental psychology

A model that has been very influential in education circles and with adult training is the model of R M Gagne. This summarises the findings of various experimental psychologists who have studied the behaviour of individuals in an experimental setting in order to understand the details of how we learn. In the sense that they studied behaviour systematically they are behaviourists but not in the strict sense of Skinner's approach. Gagne (1975) has identified a chain of eight events that occur whatever sort of learning is taking place. These are, in order:

- *motivation*. The learner has to want to learn and to want to learn this particular thing or the final product of this type of learning. For example, a manager of a hotel may be keen to learn how to manage his or her staff well and so is motivated to learn about psychology and its application in the work place.

- *perception*. The matter to be learned has to be distinguished from others. This involves identifying a clear objective. At first it is difficult because one has not learned the different categories in the area. With time one learns more and more detailed ways of classifying the matter to be learned. For example, at the beginning of this course you may wonder where to start and what it is essential to learn. After a few weeks or months many of the terms become familiar and identifiable topics that need learning become clear.

- *acquisition*. What has to be learned is related to the familiar, so that it makes sense. For example, in this book I have tried to give examples from work settings to help to make sense of a new area of study. You can help yourself by recalling your own examples from your own experience.

- *retention*. The two-stage process of human learning comprises, a short-term memory where items are stored first and a long-term memory to which they are transferred and where they are held permanently. Not everything needs to go to the long-term memory. For example, the anecdotes and jokes that aid the process of understanding at the time do not need to go to the long-term memory.

- *recall*. This is the ability to summon things up from memory when required. There are different levels. Recognition is where we know we have seen the item before and it takes less time to familiarise ourselves with it but we could not have relied on memory alone. Recall is where we can generate the memory of our own accord. For example, at the end of your course you may be able to recognise some of the material in this book as vaguely familiar: it may just seem 'common sense'. Some other parts you could recall from memory without the book because you have learnt it more thoroughly.

- *generalisation*. This is the ability to apply the learning in situations other than the specific one in which it was learned. For example, you may generalise what you learn on this course about motivation in the workplace to thinking about motivation at the sports club or in the family.

- *performance*. This is where what has been learned is put into practice. It is the test of learning. The professional management student takes the exam, writes the essay or tries to use the materials from the course at work.

- *feedback on performance*. This is where the learner finds out whether the performance was satisfactory or not. Sometimes it will be obvious because of the quality of the performance, particularly with physical skill learning such as car driving. But some feedback from the coach or trainer can help to distinguish more subtle levels of satisfaction or to analyse what went wrong, how it could be avoided, what needs more practice, what to do next and so on.

Learning can fail because of problems at any of these stages. The model is useful as a practical checklist when helping others to prepare for learning or when giving feedback at the end of a learning session. It is also a useful model for analysing more informal methods of learning, such as why some get the message at meetings and others do not.

Experiential learning

Another useful model of how people learn is that of Kolb, Rubin and McIntyre (1974). Table 3 shows their experiential learning model. In their view, all the stages are necessary if learning is to take place.

Table 3 Kolb's learning model

A cycle of:
  Concrete experience
  Reflective observation
  Abstract concepts and generalisations
  Application of ideas

The model suggests that learning is a cycle of the following stages:

- concrete experience, or experience that involves performance – for example, having a go at conducting an appraisal interview.

- observation and reflective analysis of the experience, or using listening and looking. This is most useful if done from many perspectives: in our example, discussing the appraisal interview with someone from the personnel department, the course tutor and friends with similar experience.

- generalisation on the basis of experience, or doing some thinking. Such generalisations use abstract concepts to integrate the observations into the theories we have about the world – for example, discussing with others what they would have done in the circumstances of the appraisal interview.

- experimentation in future action based on the generalisation, or doing something similar. The application of ideas requires active experimentation. In our example the next time an appraisal interview is to be conducted, either in practice or for real, possible actions could be discussed and carried out.

- new experience derived from this experimentation – in our example, getting the student to do another appraisal interview.

- initiation of a new learning cycle.

If you can imagine a spiral of these experiential learning cycles you can see how a model of continual improvement and learning could be developed with the learner becoming increasingly confident and ambitious in his or her performance and analysis. This model of learning is very popular in higher education, where there is a growing emphasis on trying to make students do something so the cycle can actually start. There is good theoretical evidence that a learner who uses different senses and actually does something is more engaged in the learning process than one who merely reads or listens. Reading and listening are the more difficult ways to learn. This model is further developed in the next section.

> Use Kolb's model to analyse your own learning. Use one of the practical sessions in your course, for example an exercise, role play, case study or visit. Which part of the activity did you find most interesting? Which was most difficult? Which part seemed irrelevant and time consuming? Now can you relate these findings to the Kolb cycle?

use this !!

Individual differences

So far we have suggested that everyone learns things in the same sort of way. This may be generally true but there are also individual differences in how we learn effectively and in how we prefer to learn. We are all aware that people differ in the speed with which they learn new things and that some learn physical skills quickly and theoretical material slowly compared with others and vice versa. However there is also some evidence that individuals differ in their preferred method of learning whatever the subject matter.

Kolb, Rubin and Osland (1991) developed the model of a learning cycle described earlier (see Table 3) to suggest that since the learning process is driven by individual needs and goals, so learning styles become highly individual in both direction and process. For example, a physicist may come to place great emphasis on abstract concepts, whereas a sculptor may value concrete experience more highly. A manager may be primarily concerned with the active application of concepts, whereas an ecologist may develop observational skills highly. Each of us will develop a personal style that has some weak points and some strong points. We may leap into experiences and fail to observe the lessons to be derived from these experiences; we may form concepts but fail to test their validity. In some areas our objectives may give us clear guidelines while in others we wander aimlessly.

Let us try to systematise this understanding a little. There are two main dimensions in the Kolb model of learning styles: a concrete-abstract dimension, 1 and 3 in the cycle, and an active-reflective dimension, 4 and 2 in the cycle. By making a grid of the four main learning processes on these two dimensions, Kolb arrived at a grid of four basic learning styles (see Figure 1).

Figure 1 Kolb's learning styles

	Active experimentation	Reflective observation
Concrete Experience	Accomodator	Diverger
Abstract conceptualisation	Converger	Assimilator

Kolb's four basic learning styles are:

- *convergent style*. The main strength of this style is in problem-solving, decision-making and the practical application of ideas. People with this style do best where there is a single answer or solution; they prefer technical rather than social and interpersonal issues.

- *divergent style*. This is the opposite of the convergent style. The great strength of this style is in imaginative ability and awareness of meaning and values. People with this style look at concrete issues from a variety of ways, and they are able to organise these into a pattern or 'Gestalt'. This style is characteristic of arts people, counsellors and personnel people.

- *assimilation style*. The great strengths here are the ability to create abstract models and to assimilate diverse material into a coherent explanation. People with this style have less concern with people and more with ideas; they tend to be researchers and planners.

- *accommodation style*. This is the opposite of assimilation and people here are good at doing things and carrying out plans. They are quick to adapt if the plan does not quite work; they simply get on with it. People with this style are most common in business and are likely to be in marketing or sales.

A variation on this learning style model is that of the British writers Honey and Mumford (1992). They used Kolb's model in a slightly different way, emphasising the particular stages of the cycle that individuals favour:

- *activists* who use concrete experience involve themselves fully and without bias in new experiences. They tend to act first and consider the consequences afterwards.

- *reflectors* who use observation and reflection are thoughtful and cautious. They like to sit back and ponder experiences.

- *theorists* who form abstract concepts integrate things into logically sound theories. They tend to be perfectionists who do not give up until everything has been fitted into a rational scheme.

- *pragmatists* who rely on generalisations actively seek out new ideas to see if they will work in practice. They like to get on with things and enjoy a challenge.

Whichever model of learning styles is used, both are useful in establishing that there are individual differences in how people learn from experience. Those responsible for learning, training and development of people must ensure that there are sufficient different learning experiences available to suit different people. The more we understand our own learning style, the more likely we are to be able to learn effectively. Just because a method works for a friend does not necessarily mean you are dumb if it does not work for you!

Using either Kolb or Honey and Mumford, what sort of learner do you think you are? What are likely to be the weaknesses of this? How could these weaknesses be overcome?

EFFECTIVE LEARNING IN DIFFERENT SITUATIONS

So far we have been looking at how people learn. This has attracted a good deal of attention, not only from school teachers but also from people involved in adult training. Another area that has been investigated is whether different sorts of learning material require different learning methods to optimise the learning. If we accept some of the generalisations of the previous section on how people learn can we fine tune them to suit different situations?

Traditionally a distinction is drawn between cognitive (intellectual) learning, learning skills and developing attitudes. Each of these is thought not only to be a different objective but also to require a different learning process. The distinction has been refined for practical use in adult learning by the Industrial Training Research Unit (1976). They took the work of Belbin to develop the CRAMP taxonomy. CRAMP divides learning into five types:

- *comprehension*. This involves learning theoretical subject matter. It is knowing how, why and when things happen. This type of learning is best done through methods that treat the whole subject as an entity, rather than splitting it up into bits and taking one at a time. This is usually achieved by lecture, seminar, discussion, film or video. Clarity of presentation is critical so that the main points are distinguished from the supporting evidence. An example of such a learning type would be the learning of mathematics.

- *reflex learning*. This is acquiring skilled movements or perceptual abilities. As well as knowledge of what to do, speed and co-ordination are at a premium; it requires practice and repetition. It is best approached by breaking the task into small steps and simplifying each step so that it can be easily learned. Even a simple piece of behaviour can actually be very complicated. Breaking a task into smaller steps is called 'task analysis' by behaviourist psychologists. If we get smaller steps right we have the opportunity to be rewarded. If the steps are too big success is unlikely and there is no opportunity for reward and so learning does not take place readily. An example would be using a new piece of equipment, machining materials, inspecting goods for quality problems or typing.

- *attitude development.* This enables people to change their attitudes and social skills. It is perhaps the most difficult sort of learning to achieve. Group methods that centre on people knowing themselves seem the most effective as attitudes are very difficult to influence in other ways. One example would be a customer care course where the attitude of staff is explored by encouraging them to discuss their behaviour after doing an exercise such as 'finding the treasure' in a park. It is hoped that this will lead them to a better understanding of themselves and that through such self-knowledge they will arrive at a better position from which to change their behaviour towards customers.

- *memory training.* This is learning information by heart. It is very similar to reflex learning, where each bit is taken one at a time. All sorts of jingles and mnemonics can be helpful here; you will frequently see mnemonics such as CRAMP in student texts. Obvious examples are actors learning their lines in a play or medical students learning the names of the bones in the body.

- *procedural learning.* This is similar to memory training but the items do not need to be memorised only understood and their location known. This requires less practice. Examples are a lawyer's knowledge of the statutes or an engineer's knowledge of how to shut the plant down for maintenance. Neither would need to know by heart what to do but both would need to know where to look and to understand what they found. You have probably by now learnt to use your academic library. If you came to visit another you would know more or less how to use it but would probably need a few minutes in which to orientate yourself and to find the references that you need.

In practice most learning situations require more than one of these types of learning but the categorisation is a helpful means of sorting out which would be the most appropriate means of learning something. For example, in professional exams there are some things that need to be learned by heart, others that one needs to have some understanding of and others where procedural learning would be most appropriate. The most effective learners are those who can classify their needs and do not waste time memorising everything.

What types of learning would be most effective if you wanted to do the following:

use the CD-Rom to seek references for an assignment; become influential in a political party; understand organisational behaviour; understand a balance sheet in a company's annual report?

ROLE THEORY

We have been looking at learning from a psychologist's point of view. The sociologist's perspective on learning is to concentrate on how and why people come to belong to a group. Sociologists seek to understand the reasons behind the behaviours studied by psychologists. Only by explaining people's understandings of a situation and the methods they use to organise their attitudes and knowledge – that is their orientation – will we fully understand social relationships. We need to understand the meanings of actions. Why do people want to learn particular things? Why and how do they become part of the group? Which things help and which hinder membership?

One very useful concept in understanding these sorts of questions is that of 'role'. The term role describes some of the effects of the continuing process of social learning. In our various roles we are driven by the pressures to learn appropriate behaviours and values in order to conform to the differing groups to which we belong, or wish to belong. This concept is used very similarly to the use of the word in drama: it describes the social interaction rather than the specific person. Role-playing is action in conformity with a set of social rules. These social rules will be based on expectations and obligations derived from the social or cultural values of a particular setting. Any one person may have a unique set of roles to play. These personal collections of roles can come into conflict and a choice has to be made between them. For example, your lecturers may have formal expectations that require them to be teachers, writers, counsellors, researchers and administrators; they will have to choose which is the most important role when time is short.

The different roles we play are often defined by the institutions to which we belong – such as families, communities or religious groups. These institutions set norms – that is, they set expectations and obligations that go to make up a role. Business organisations are one such institution that set norms for various roles. These roles in turn make up the structure of the organisation or institution.

The concepts commonly used to describe roles and social learning – or socialisation – are given below, with some explanations:

- role – set of expectations and obligations to act in specific ways in particular settings

- status – an actor's position in a social structure which limits the roles to be played

- social structure – the organisation of role, status and social institutions into a determining pattern

- institution – well established orientations, values and norms in stable patterns

- norm – the normal standards of behaviour that define a role

- primary group – a small, intimate group such as family, gang, group of close workmates; an important source of norms and values for individual members

- reference group – social groups that provide the norms for people who want to belong to them

- significant other – a role model that the individual initially imitates in order to become part of the group that is 'socialised'

- generalised other – where an individual takes into account the other roles within a group and makes his or her own adaptation to them.

This gives us the conceptual framework to look at various social relationships and how we adapt to them. It is a different way of looking at learning from that of psychology.

> Who is in your primary group at work? What norms of behaviour do you have? What behaviours did you change when you arrived in the group?

THE LEARNING ORGANISATION

Dealing with change has attracted a lot of attention from managerial writers and they tend to describe organisations that cope well as 'learning organisations'. The idea of a learning organisation was first articulated by Argyris and Schon (1978) and developed by people such as Morgan (1986) and Pedlar, Burgoyne and Boydell (1991). The last group are influential British writers on training and development. Various lists, probably not quite well established enough yet to call them models, have been developed to describe these 'learning organisations'.

According to Marquand and Reynolds (1994) a manager wishing to build his or her organisation's capacity to learn should attempt to:

- transform the individual and organisation's image of learning with the aim of encouraging life-long learning and a desire for continuous improvement

- create knowledge-based partnerships with people within and without the organisation in order to share ideas and information so that a real understanding develops

- develop and expand team-learning activities in order to encourage people to share questions, information, ideas, solutions and approaches

- change the role of managers so that they function as facilitators rather than controllers

- encourage experiments and risk-taking so that new possibilities emerge

- create structures and systems that allow people time to extract learning – this suggests provision of some 'soft' time for people to talk and develop

- build opportunities and mechanisms in order to disseminate learning both formally and informally

- empower people to take decisions and actions

- push information through the organisation and to external associates

- develop the discipline of system thinking – what are the implications for others?

- develop a powerful vision of organisational excellence and individual fulfilment

- root out bureaucracy.

Pedlar, Burgoyne and Boydell (1991) suggest that the following features are indicative of a learning organisation, although they prefer the term learning company to learning organisation:

- a learning approach to strategy – risks are taken and new opportunities tried, people learn about the new as well as the well established

- participative policy-making with consultation and participation by people from all parts of the organisation

- open information systems – nothing is hidden from members of the organisation unless it is imperative that it be hidden

- formative accounting and control – which encourages people – rather than restrictive methods

- internal exchange of ideas and information

- flexibility of rewards so people can work to their own best way

- structures that make individual contributions possible

- capacity for boundary workers to act as boundary scanners

- inter-worker learning

- a learning climate for all

- self-development opportunities for all.

Some of these ideas are frankly rather idealistic. These lists can seem a list of wishes rather than a practical guide to the reality of most organisations. Many would feel that they are not only unworkable but also potentially damaging to the viability of the organisation. However, the advantages of the idea of the learning organisation is that it can be a useful checklist for raising questions about an existing organisation. It is rather difficult to see how you could set out with this as an indication of how to do it. By taking each of the concepts as a question we can ask how a particular organisation does things. If these ways are felt to be restricting then ideas from the learning-organisation approach have the advantage of opening up the discussion and using all the talents available to the organisation rather than simply relying on those at the top. In a competitive world those close to the customer are more likely to know what is really needed.

The concept of the learning organisation has obvious similarities with some of the underpinning ideas of Total Quality Management (TQM) and the Business Process Re-engineering (BPR) – ideas with an emphasis on continuous improvement, breaking down barriers, customer supply chains and empowerment. The useful aspect of these views are that they look at the organisation as a whole and at how various functions and specialisms relate to one another. One way of looking at the learning-organisation models is to see them as integrating models of managing people.

This chapter has emphasised models of different learning styles, objectives and roles concerned with the individual. By now you should be aware that learning is not just a simple mechanical process. This concern with learning and the different models that can be used to analyse learning has now been applied to the whole organisation and the idea of a learning organisation has been the subject of much interest over the last few years. The issue of learning is currently at the heart of much discussion on managing people and so reoccurs in other chapters in this book, particularly Chapter 9.

AND FINALLY...

What would you recommend Laura do? Would any of the models in this chapter be useful? I would probably suggest looking at the individual styles of the members of staff as the nature of the service offered is one of personal, individual attention. Emphasising individuals would make some sense. The Kolb or Honey and Mumford approach would seem appropriate.

FURTHER READING

The chapter on learning in either Kolb *et al* (1974) or Kolb *et al* (1991) will give you further details of their views. I particularly like the 1991 book as it offers many exercises including one on discovering your own learning style. For more on roles look at any introductory text on sociology. There are innumerable books about the change process in organisations. Pedlar, Burgoyne and Boydell (1991) is particularly well regarded in the United Kingdom.

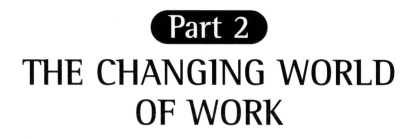

Part 2
THE CHANGING WORLD OF WORK

4 Factors influencing work, jobs and employment opportunities

OBJECTIVES

By the time you have read this chapter you should be able to:

- understand and explain the context in which organisations have to make decisions about the nature of employment

- understand and explain the psychological contract of employment.

DAVID'S CHOICE OF MANAGEMENT STYLES

David was chief executive of a waste management company. In the previous two years a raft of legislation had changed the nature of what could and could not be put into the landfill sites that the company owned and managed. The way in which the materials were handled and the documentation that went with it had also changed dramatically. Many of the employees who had worked for the organisation for a long time could not see the point of all this form filling and were loathe to wear all the 'sissy' protective clothing that the company issued. What should David do?

Should he sack a token member of staff to show how serious he was? Increase the random inspections? Hope no one noticed the lapses in procedures? Offer incentives for filling in the forms and wearing the clothing? Give pep talks to the site managers? Was there a need for firm action or encouraging compliance? Would his actions change the nature of the relationship between the organisation and those who worked for it?

The dilemma for people managing in organisations is that the flexibility of what can be done is often influenced by events outside their own control and even outside that of the organisation. These outside influences can also affect the very nature of the employment relationship. This chapter looks at the influences that affect the employment relationship. This relationship can give rise to conflict and co-operation, confusion and contradiction – and a variety of power distributions. The influence of the wider context on the relationship is mediated by the particular ways in which members of an organisation interact with each other.

THE EMPLOYMENT ENVIRONMENT

A popular framework for summarising the outside factors that can influence the employment relationship is PEST – see, for example, Marchington and Wilkinson (1996, p8). According to this framework, the following are the main outside factors:

- *political/legal* – government stability, attitudes towards the European Union, employment and other legislation

- *economic* – stages in the business cycle, unemployment, inflation, interest rates

- *social* – population changes, income distribution, education and training, attitudes to work and leisure

- *technological* – new discoveries and development, government spending on and promotion of research, speed of technological transfer.

All of these can affect the nature of the employment relationship. Let us look at each briefly.

The attitude of politicians towards organisations and their employees varies across political perspectives and time. Historically this is best seen in the attitude to the trade union movement in the United Kingdom. One of the first priorities of the Conservative administration of Mrs Thatcher in the early 1980s was to introduce legislation covering strikes and ballots. Other legislation that affected the employment relationship includes the Factory Acts of the first half of the nineteenth century, covering the conditions of work, and employment law covering rights to time off work, termination of employment, guarantee of minimum pay and rights of part-time staff. For many these are seen as a 'floor' of rights, a minimum that employees should expect. Many, but not all, employers give better conditions than the minimum. Other political issues like the introduction of the 'Euro' will affect the work of people – particularly if you are a currency trader and you lose your job.

How the economy is doing affects the optimism of organisations and determines whether they invest in more staff, higher salaries and new ventures. These decisions in turn affect the actual work that individuals do as well as how many workers there are and what they are paid. Working for an expanding business is exciting and encourages innovation and risk. Money is available to develop ideas and everyone moves on. In contrast a declining market can mean trying to preserve what one has and requires the diplomatic skills of an angel when explaining to staff that their wonderful idea for an improvement cannot be afforded. This will include aspects of the global economy as well. After decades of the economies of South East Asia, the so-called 'Tiger economies', being held up as paragons of virtue it was quite a shock to many working in the West when these tiger economies experienced sharp declines at the end of the 1990s. It affected those in the West, as well, as there was a reduction in demand for many exported goods and fewer tourists travelled from East to West. The globalisation of the economy has meant the employment relationship is now affected by global events even for those who work in locally based concerns.

Globalisation is the process whereby the business environment has become increasingly international or global. One aspect derives from the improvements in telecommunications that have enabled call centres to answer queries about such things as financial matters or airline bookings to be based anywhere in the world. Another aspect is increasing competition from other countries that can offer services more cheaply. For example, the software prowess of India has led to job losses in Europe as solutions are found online from India. Increasingly, large multinational organisations set the pace in their industries with little regard for national practices and traditions. Globalisation also means organisations employing people from other countries to work alongside locals. This is particularly true in Europe with the free movement of people within the European Union for employment. Most of us will be affected by some aspect of these global trends even if we feel we are working in a very small local organisation. For many, staying in the office late in order to talk to New York is normal. Certainly we have all experienced the slowing down in the working of the Internet in the afternoon as Americans wake up and log on!

Whether there is a shortage or surplus of appropriately skilled people will affect how much organisations are prepared to invest in their current staff. When there is a shortage, or one is predicted, it is worth their while to train and develop new, skilled people. When there are plenty looking for jobs, they do not need to do so. The attractions of many areas in Britain to new investors derives from the fact that there is a ready-made skilled workforce waiting.

New technologies affect the number and nature of the people required, and where there is a shortage of appropriate people there will again be a change in the balance of power between the employer and the employee. The expected problem of the change from the year 1999 to 2000 for computers is, at the time of writing, ensuring that those who can deal with the problem are in great demand. Were it possible to buy a CD that dealt with all the problems, then these people would no longer be quite so fêted.

> What outside influences in the PEST terminology most affect your work? What do you do to keep up to date about this?

Technological innovation
Changes in machines, equipment processes and work layout affect our work, as do the actual methods, systems and procedures involved in carrying out the work. Both of these can affect the following:

- the specific design of a particular job – the nature and variety of activities and the degree of autonomy for any particular worker

- the physical mobility of those doing a task and whether they work in groups or not will affect the relationships they have with each other

- the difficulty of acquiring a particular skill will affect the status and pay of the operator

- the people may require special clothing or physical skills.

Managing change when new technology is introduced is important as you may not only be asking the workers to work differently but the technology may also be affecting the nature of their relationships with each other. For example, the move to teleworking at home has meant that many members of staff are isolated from the casual gossip at the photocopier and coffee machine that many enjoy, so weekly Friday lunchtime meetings are set up to bring everyone together.

A more detailed example of the effect of new technology on work and working relationships was reported in *People Management* (9.10.1997, p44). The Scottish Office in Glasgow experimented with a variety of new ways of working. They had a staff of 70, in four teams, in a third of the space previously occupied. The aim was to create an efficient, effective and creative workplace. They used office design, technology, changes in working practices and the workplace culture to try to achieve this. They set up the following:

- virtual telephone numbers that followed the individual at home/commuting /office

- plug-ins for laptops all over the office

- video-conferencing facilities

- wire-free work places for quiet work

- shared space so no one had their own spot

- hot work space/desks/worktops/cubicles/offices – all bookable

- soft areas for discussions, such as a café

- meeting areas for more formal discussions.

This led to a status-free, creative, productive, knowledge-sharing output rather than an input culture. The emphasis changed from what people did to what they achieved. When the scheme was assessed they found the following:

- productivity was increased and not dominated by presenteeism

- creativity declined, as only those who were previously known got involved – the new environment was difficult for newcomers to become known.

- communication declined – due to a similar problem as that restricting creativity

- esteem was liked by the participants but resisted by others in the organisation.

> Which aspects of your work determines how and where you work? Would you want to do it differently? How easy is it for the newcomer to fit in?

CUSTOMER AND CONSUMER EXPECTATIONS

There are two sorts of customers: those who themselves have customers, and the end-users best described as consumers. Let us look at the effect of customer expectations first.

Customers will influence what is provided by their specifications for a service or product. The nature of a contract or sale will affect when and what is provided. Increasingly, however, customers are also influencing *how* things are done because they are required to comply with various standards. Influences from customers can take the form of pressure to conform to particular standards and be accredited in order that the customers' own accreditation is in place for *their* customers. This may concern Quality Assurance, Investors In People or environmental auditing. Each of these standards will affect how work is done and the amount of paperwork needed to track each stage of a procedure. There is a change in the nature of the trust that is expressed in that those who require things to be written down are giving a slightly different message from those who do not. Many of these sorts of procedure enable organisations to prove that procedures have been complied with should a query arise. They are an inevitable consequence of the increasing cultural emphasis on 'blame'.

Another influence on the nature of the work that we do is the expectation of consumers. The effect of the green lobby is perhaps the most graphic of these in the impact that has been made on pollution controls and recycling packaging. An incentive is given to organisations to meet the generally felt standards of acceptable environmental practice. When Shell wanted to dispose of the Brent Spar oil platform at the end of its practical life in the early–mid 1990s they planned to sink it deep in the Atlantic Ocean. They consulted the various statutory and professional bodies about their plan, but they completely failed to consult environmental groups and they did not try to take the public along with them. Although the technical evidence was supportive of their position they had completely failed to take account of the beliefs and emotions of the general population – particularly in Germany – about the need to preserve the wildness of the ocean bed. Consequently, Shell had to back off and reorganise the whole decision-making about Brent Spar's disposal. The understanding of the organisational context by senior management has changed completely in the light of this case. Now the consumer and general population are considered too.

Organisations need to be customer-orientated for obvious reasons. If they do not meet precisely the customer's needs then someone else will. Competition is always there. Being close to the customer enables organisations to pick up on nuances of change and to adapt gradually to these – rather than doing nothing until they find they are so far out of touch that the necessary change is impossibly big. Keeping close to the customer is important for all members of an organisation, including human resources staff who need to know how the employment market is changing and what the HRM implications are of business changes. For example, when the economic cycle is booming keeping hold of staff may be an issue and ensuring sufficiently trained staff are available for expansion is important. When there is a depression in the cycle, however, the priority is to keep employment costs down whilst ensuring that critical skills and competencies remain available within the staff.

> What do you do because your customers/consumers ask you to? How do you find out what they want?

THE EMPLOYMENT RELATIONSHIP

The relationship between employers and their employees can be described in many ways. Any relationship is formed within a context of rights, expectations and obligations on the part of each party to it. Some of these are unspoken, in others there is a need for negotiation. Other aspects have a legal framework that imposes obligations and guarantees rights. Relationships are also influenced by cultural norms of what is and what is not acceptable about the balance of power.

As Foot and Hook (1996, p140) point out, the general feeling in the industrial relations arena in the 1990s is that the balance of power lies with the employer. High levels of unemployment, the restrictions on Trade Unions and redundancies have reduced people's feelings of job security. This has led to the development of more individual relationships between managers and their staff over such things as the nature of trust, openness, willingness to co-operate and acceptance of different points of view. Where there are big differences of power these are more difficult to establish and managers have to work harder to assure their staff that they matter – as we will see in more detail in the chapters on leadership (Chapter 10) and influencing (Chapter 11).

The balance between the organisation and the individual has been summed up in the phrase 'psychological contract'. This phrase was first used by Mumford (1972) and has since been frequently used by writers on personnel management and human resource management. The psychological contract is like the implied terms of a legal contract – much of it is assumed and unspoken. It includes factors that affect feelings, motivation and loyalty. It itself is affected by the climate of the organisation and the nature of management style, which can be coercive or co-operative or a calculated style in the middle – see Etzioni's description of this in Chapter 7. Employees differ as much as their managers in their understanding of the contract. The psychological contract between employers and the employed in the past was a job for life in return for your effort. The new-style contract is lifelong employability in exchange for your effort. The employer is offering development, experience and maintaining a currency with modern events and methods. All of which are invaluable when seeking employment.

As Herriot and Pemberton (1995) point out, the concept of a contract requires two people and in reality the employers are usually bullying the employees to accept what is on offer. Their model of the balance between organisations and individuals suggests that there are various dimensions in which the contract between the individual and an organisation can be negotiated. Figure 2 is based on some of Herriot and Pemberton's ideas.

Figure 2 The balance between organisations and individuals

	ORGANISATION		INDIVIDUAL
Employment	Organisation career	Negotiates over time	Job for now
Development	Integrated career		Job training
Responsibility	Organisation ⟶	Partnership ⟵	Individual

The concept of employability
If the psychological contract between employers and employees no longer offers security of employment in one organisation job security will have to depend on our ability to be employable. Kanter (1989) argued the point that job security was each person's employability.

Employement securite
Employabilite

If security no longer comes from being employed, then it must come from being employable. In a post-entrepreneurial era in which corporations need flexibility to change and restructuring is a fact of life, the promise of very long term employment security would be the wrong one to expect employers to make. But employment security – the knowledge that today's work will enhance the person's value in terms of future opportunities – that is a promise that can be made and kept. Employability security comes from the chance to accumulate human capital – skills and reputation – that can be invested in new opportunities as they arise.

(Kanter 1989, p321)

If Kanter is right, it suggests that individuals should constantly keep up to date with skills and knowledge and learn to learn. She also implies that organisations and their managers will need employees who can take on new ideas and techniques and adapt to situations which match their core activities, and will need to encourage individuals to take on these challenges. This concept of employability is increasingly understood by individuals. One young programmer I know who works on contract will take contracts only in the up-and-coming languages to ensure his future; any that are offered in older languages he refuses, even if it means having a few days or weeks out of work. This in turn has implications for the organisations that have older processes and procedures: they will be seen as less favourable opportunities by the ambitious workers.

Associated with this contract is the idea of the added value worker. This suggests that each person must add value to the organisation and to those who work with them, and this value should exceed the employee's cost. If people do not add value and are not improving they are at risk of losing their jobs. In turn the employer is expected to make expectations clear, offer opportunities for training and development and give honest feedback.

This concept of adding value as an employee suggests an individual accountability to contribute to the enterprise. As we will see when looking at poor performance in the final chapter, an individual 's contribution will be effective only if his or her personal characteristics and the organisational characteristics are well suited. Sometimes there are problems on one side, sometimes on the other. In many ways this book tries to encourage individuals to contribute and add value by ensuring that a suitable organisational climate exists for them to do so.

This chapter has looked at some of the factors that affect the work available for people to do in organisations. The relationship that develops between the individual and the organisation will depend on these and other internal factors that can be summed as the psychological contract of employment. The final part of this book explores the nature of this contract in more detail.

AND FINALLY...

What would you do about the reluctant workers at David's company? Would anything here help? I think I would consider the psychological contract and the nature of the relationship that exists Changing the culture of an organisation takes a lot of time and effort and perhaps David has to start by emphasising the changing world outside the organisation. He may need to be tough with some of the individuals if they do not heed training and supervisory demands for compliance with regulations. In times of rapid change a combination of persuasive leadership and controls is often used. Part 3 of this book returns to this theme.

FURTHER READING

Farnham (1999) on the business context has sections on the economy, political system, social structure, legal framework, technology and international factors. Chapter 6 of Foot and Hook (1996) deals with the psychological contract and the legal aspects of the employment contract.

5 Differing work patterns

OBJECTIVES

When you have finished reading this chapter you should be able to:

- describe ways of redesigning jobs

- understand and explain differing types of employment and work patterns.

JANICE'S REQUEST

Janice is 33. She has been working for her boss for three years and has been with the firm for the last six years. Her work has always been acceptable but not exceptional. She has just come back from maternity leave and asks her boss whether it would be possible for her to work part-time or on a job share for the next few years until her child is old enough to go to school. What do you think her boss needs to think about before giving her an answer?

Should Janice's boss consult colleagues? Does her boss need to look at the precise nature of the work she does before deciding? Would some tasks be easier to operate part-time than others? Is there a problem about which hours/days? Is there an issue of fair play? What are the implications for those who work alongside Janice? Is this an opportunity to 'lose' Janice and hope for a 'more committed' replacement? Is there another member of staff who would like to job share?

Many of us find ourselves in organisations that are reorganising departments and teams by changing the numbers, skill mix and organisation of staff including increasingly using contract or part-time staff. We are also individually choosing to balance our lives between work and other aspects of life in a variety of ways. It is very important, from the organisation's point of view, that someone knows what work needs doing. The work to be done needs organising into coherent jobs, into a structure that enables workers to communicate and liaise with each other. This task usually falls to the line manager, as he or she is expected to know – and often is the only person in a position to know – precisely the nature of the tasks that need doing day to day. This is the heart of operational management.

In general terms there are five main steps that need thinking about:

- *purpose* – what purpose in the organisation will the department, section or team serve? Does it provide a service to others in the organisation or deal directly with customers? Does it co-ordinate others' activities or serve some other purpose?

- *activities* – what activities are needed to fulfil the purpose? What are the essential things to be done? This is not necessarily everything that is currently being done and may include new tasks.

- *job design* – how are the activities best grouped into jobs? Which of the above activities are best done by one person because of the expertise or access to others that is required? Are some jobs best done by everyone because they keep everyone in touch with each other? This is dealt with in more detail later.

- *authority* – what formal authority do the job holders need to have delegated to them?

- *connections* – how can the activities of the job holders be connected through information systems and reporting?

The above questions are the starting points for considering what people are asked to do at work. Having a clear view of the task to be done is important – see Chapter 14 on performance management. But there are other issues to be considered.

JOB DESIGN

Ensuring that everyone has a suitable job has been one of the enduring themes of management thought and writing. This is usually called job design although actually it is more often a case of job redesign. It is the process of getting the optimum fit between what the organisation requires of the individual employee and the individual's need for satisfaction in the job. This can either be done by 'dumbing down' jobs so that anyone can do them and then using a carrot and stick method, or it can be a 'holistic' approach of trying to motivate people to develop themselves and the job.

widud

Hackman (1987) suggests there are various dimensions in jobs associated with good performance by the job holder. Table 4 shows the five characteristics identified by Hackman. We might want to add the following based on the human relations models:

- dealing with others – how much staff have to deal with other people will vary and different amounts suit different people

- friendship opportunities – establishing informal relationships at work is of varying importance to different people.

These dimensions give meaning to work, and to the job-holders give responsibility and knowledge of how they are doing. By taking various actions – see Table 5 – motivation and performance can in this model be improved.

As an example of how these characteristics work, many of the ideas have been incorporated in the concept of individual team members having their own customers. For example in hospitals where patients have a named nurse, not only does the patient know who is his or her carer but the nurses get some of the characteristics shown in Table 4 in their working day.

Jobs redesign strategy

Several different ways of improving job satisfaction through redesign have been tried. The major ways of redesigning, or designing, jobs that have been described are:

- *job rotation* – moving from one job to another to reduce boredom and increase skills. For example, in one chemical factory the operators are moved around between receiving goods from suppliers, checking the process, running the process and packing the final product ready for transport to their customers.

- *job enlargement* – increase the number of tasks done by an individual. For example, the waiting staff at the restaurant

Table 4 **Job dimensions and their effects**

1 *Skill variety*. The way a job demands a variety of different activities that involve using a number of different skills and talents.	These give meaning to the work people do.
2 *Task identity*. The way a job requires the job-holder to complete a whole and coherent piece of work having a tangible outcome.	
3 *Task significance*. The way a job has an impact on the lives or work of other people, inside the organisation or outside.	
4 *Autonomy*. The way a job-holder enjoys freedom from supervision, independence and discretion in deciding how the job should be done.	This gives responsibility to job-holders.
5 *Feedback*. The way the job-holder receives clear and direct information about his or her effectiveness.	This gives the job-holder knowledge of results.

Source: Adapted from J.R. Hackman, 'Work design', in *Motivation and Work Behaviour*, ed. R.M. Steers *and* L.W. Porter, London, McGraw-Hill, 1989

Table 5 **Ways of getting good results on the five job descriptions**

Action	Job dimension affected
1 *Forming natural work units* so that the work to be done has a logic and makes sense to the job-holder.	2, 3
2 *Combining tasks* so that a number of natural work units may be put together to make a bigger and more coherent job.	1, 2
3 *Establishing links with clients* so that the job-holder has contact with people using the service or product the job-holder is supplying.	1, 4, 5
4 *Vertical loading* so that job-holders take on more of the management of their jobs in deciding what to do, organising their own time, solving their own problems and controlling their own costs.	4
5 *Opening feedback channels* so that job-holders can discover more about how they are doing and whether their performance is improving or deteriorating.	5

Adapted from Hackman (1987)

chain TGI Fridays are expected to entertain and 'host' the customers at their tables. The job is larger than just taking orders, serving meals and clearing dishes.

- *job enrichment* – broaden the responsibilities and increase individual autonomy for decision-making. For example, hotel reception staff can negotiate the price charged for a room that night and work out a suitable package rather than having to keep to a set price and lose the customer.

- *autonomous work teams* – where the team decides how, when and for how much the work is done. This requires a skilled team and for management to be prepared to let go. It has been less common in the United Kingdom than in the USA and Scandinavia.

- *leadership models* – where the vision of the leader is sufficient to give meaning and significance to everyone, jobs can feel more worthwhile. It is, however, difficult to achieve most of this – see Chapter 10.

- *quality movement* – this concentrates on the process of the work rather than the people, but assumes that people will be challenged by the need for constant improvement.

- *flexibility* – where people work non-traditional hours. This is discussed in detail later in this chapter.

All of these can be used successfully at team, section or departmental level. However, they can also all feel very manipulative if staff are suspicious, feeling aggrieved over pay and conditions or are left feeling uncertain about their personal futures. Like all change, it needs careful management and implementation.

None of the above will be terribly effective if the department, section or unit is poorly organised and has poor structures. Table 6 gives a checklist for reviewing the organisation of a team, section or department taken from Torrington and Weightman (1989).

Table 6 Checklist for reviewing the organisation of your department or section

Step 1 The *purpose* of the department or section

(a) Does it meet a basic business need, like purchasing or providing, or is it intended to make things run more smoothly, like personnel? Is it necessary?

(b) Is it set up on the basis of output, like business objectives to be achieved, or on the basis of inputs, like people and problems? Are the outputs already being produced elsewhere?

(c) Does the department exist to deal with matters that other managers find uninteresting or unattractive? If 'yes', are the reasons good enough?

Step 2 The *activities* to meet the purpose

(a) Does the section bring together those who share a particular skill or those with a particular responsibility?

(b) What activities have to be carried out to meet the purpose?

(c) How many people with what experience and qualifications are needed for those activities?

(d) How many ancillary staff are needed? How can that number be reduced? How can that number be reduced further?

(e) Are all the identified activities needed? Is there any duplication with other sections and departments? Is there a better way?

Step 3 *Grouping* the activities

(a) How much specialisation is needed? How will this specialisation affect job satisfaction, commitment and efficiency?

(b) Are boundaries between jobs clearly defined and in the right place?

(c) Will job-holders have the amount of discretion needed to be effective?

Step 4 The *authority* of job-holders

(a) Do job titles and other 'labels' indicate satisfactorily what authority the job-holder has?

(b) Do all job-holders have the necessary equipment – like keys, computer codes, and information – for their duties?

(c) Do all job-holders have the required authorisations – like authorisation to sign documents – that are needed?

(d) Is the authority of any job-holder unreasonably restricted?

Continued overleaf

Step 5 *Connecting* the activities of job-holders

(a) Do job-holders know what they need to know about the activities of their colleagues?

(b) Are there enough meetings of staff, too few, or too many?

(c) Are there enough copies of memoranda circulated for information, too few, or too many?

(d) Are job-holders physically located in relation to one another in a way that assists communication between those who need frequently to exchange information?

Source: Torrington and Weightman (1989)

Competency approaches to job design

There has been considerable interest in designing jobs around competencies following the national initiatives on competencies and NVQs. The design of jobs in this approach is based on analysing exactly what is required in terms of performance and then specifying the competencies required to achieve this performance and the level and standard required.

The advantages claimed for this sort of approach is that it is:

* employment-led – it is about what people actually need to do

* based on the skills needed

* outcome-led – expressed in terms of things achieved

* related to national qualifications for work-based competencies.

The difficulties can be:

* Outcomes are not always easy to specify in these terms.

* It can be difficult to keep standards low enough and not over-specify jobs.

* Competency analysis can become a complex system that is an end in itself.

* It can be difficult to determine how often competencies should be measured.

> Are there any jobs in your team/section/department that could do
> with being revamped? Would any of the above approaches help?

Different work patterns

Flexibility has become a major redesign tool for organisations.
It has various meanings and implications:

- It usually refers to the hours worked – which is discussed below.

- It can also mean functional flexibility where people can be
  moved around through increased training and relaxation of
  job demarcations.

- Numerical flexibility allows the numbers employed to
  fluctuate.

- Financial flexibility allows the employment costs to reflect
  the demand and supply of people by varying the pay given to
  people.

One way of giving people greater freedom and control over their
work is flexible working hours or flexitime. This usually means
that there is a core time when everyone must be at work and
then an agreed minimum hours per month to be achieved.
Technological changes have meant this can be extended to include
people working at home, or teleworking. This in turn has led to
the use of flexibility by employers to develop core and periphery
staff. The core staff are full-time and the periphery are called in
when required. For example, most retail organisations have part-
time staff to cover the busy times – indeed, many shops only
have part-time staff.

Here are two examples of companies using flexibility in an
attempt to meet both staff and organisational needs:

- British Airways have 33 per cent and 50 per cent contracts for
  their cabin staff as well as full-time posts. People on such
  contracts work one month in three or one in two, with the
  normal rota of off and on days. This allows staff to have whole
  months on and off, while also enabling those managing the
  rotas to treat everyone equally within a month.

work- life balance

Lilly Industries have a 'worklife programme' which includes the following options:

- part-time working – of varying lengths

- job shares – for two people to share the same full-time job

- teleworking – people work from home

- term-time working – people work only when their children are at school

- paid paternity leave – for fathers in the first year of a child's life

- career breaks – for parental care

- sabbaticals – for a variety of reasons

- periods of reduced hours – again for a variety of personal reasons.

Part of the options for staff also include health insurance, share options and pensions.

The aim is to retain skilled staff in whom the organisation has invested through training and experience, to deal with skill shortages, to lower sickness rates and to reduce 'burn-out' and enhance recruitment.

These examples show how flexibility in job design, and particularly in job hours, can benefit both employers and employees. However, not all such schemes are so equally balanced. Flexibility is too often a one-sided bargain with intolerable insecurity for individuals who are having to take on the risks of the organisations. An example is the zero-hours contract under which there is no guaranteed work or income. Others are those of full-time staff who are compulsorily made part-time or of employees forced to become self-employed, with the loss of their unfair dismissal and redundancy rights. All these have been common practice in British organisations in the 1990s. These practices may help the short-term survival of the organisation and enhance profits but they do little to engender commitment over the long term.

Do you have any flexible working? Should you have it? Whom does it benefit? What are the problems with it?

THE PERSONNEL OR HUMAN RESOURCE MANAGEMENT APPROACH

Organisation and job design is really part of the whole planning process. A development of the classic approach to planning has been to integrate th   ' for people with the planning of the organisation's goa¹   -es. This planning is done at a senior level, but c   or initiative is decided it will certainly in·   ·to propose possible ways of puttin·   · may include ideas of impr   ¿ing staffing costs, impr¢   ⅃ucts.

Approach   ⅃ctional or team basis as   ₒle, the common target ¢   , by:

- im·   .hat there are better
  e·

-

- u⌐   ₁uals better

- rewardinₒ   .y

- having annual hoᵤ   ⅃n paying for overtime.

Any of these might be effec⌐ ⅃ at reducing staffing costs on a unit, section or team basis.

This chapter is about the various aspects of ensuring that jobs are designed appropriately. There is also a need to ensure that there is adequate staffing for work to be done in the section or department. At the strategic level – that of the whole organisation – this would be a major aspect of the function of the personnel department and of top management. There is also an increasing expectation that the line manager is involved in human resource management, as it is only at this level that particular decisions about what is needed can be integrated with the development of the particular activities, or business, of the team, section and department. The team leader or department manager is best placed to do all the prior analysis about the workloads, work methods and practices that will affect the number and expertise of staff required.

Planning to have the right sort of people to do the job
One classic approach to these issues has been human resource planning, where an attempt is made to see whether there is likely to be a mismatch between the future needs of the organisation and the supply of suitably qualified and experienced staff. This is usually done by:

- scanning the horizon to see what likely changes are coming up and what are the implications for staffing. This involves looking at the organisation's plans, government action, trends in techniques, technologies and approaches to the task involved. Any of these might affect the nature of the work to be done in the department and consequently the number and nature of staff required. For example, in hospitals the rise of less intrusive surgery has led to more day cases and fewer overnight stays – with obvious changes in staffing levels required on the wards at night. These changes need to be put alongside the demand for labour within the organisation due to current practice and future plans for contraction or expansion of the service.

- examining the supply of labour within the organisation in terms of age, experience, qualifications, pay and conditions and performance of existing staff. The external supply of labour will vary depending on changes in the population, competition for workers from other organisations and the education and training available for people to qualify in particular areas.

- making a comparison between the demand and supply of staff. This forecast is the basis for planning for the future. Matching supply and demand can be done manually or by computer. Except for the simplest cases the personnel department should have access to some sophisticated, information systems using payroll and personnel information. The figures forecast are not an absolute, nor are the outcomes, as they can be influenced by interdepartmental relations, organisational politics and the empire building of senior managers. The figures will also be affected by artificial restraints from top management, as Rothwell (1995, p171) points out. For example, the board may have put a cost limit or a headcount limit for the organisation. This will affect estimates of labour demand. There will also be arguments about how these costs are counted. Does labour include only the salary or the total employment costs? Are heads counted as actual numbers or full-time equivalents?

Once there are plans and a human resource forecast, Bramham (1989, p155) suggests that the forecast allows plans to be made. Some of the areas to ask questions about and plan for are as follows. They are listed in alphabetical order:

- Accommodation – is there a need for more or fewer rooms, desks etc?

- Costs – where is there a need for additional/fewer resources?

- Culture – how are the changes going to affect the way people interact?

- Development – will there be different opportunities for staff development?

- Industrial relations – how will the unions react to the changes?

- Organisation Development – do reporting relationships need to be changed or reorganised?

- Outplacements – will some people need to find new jobs?

- Promotion – what opportunities for promotion will there be?

- Productivity – will these changes affect the amount of work each person can sensibly do?

- Recruitment – what sort of people will need to be recruited?

- Redundancy – which groups are likely to face redundancy and how is this going to be handled?

- Retirement – is there a need to change the ages at which retirement is offered?

- Reward systems – should the salary structures be changed?

- Training and retraining – which areas need to develop new skills?

- Transfer – should the transfer of staff be voluntary or compulsory?

- Working practices – is there a need to rethink the way of working?

Decisions and practice about all of these can affect the utilisation of people at work. Decisions about each of these will also affect how much work gets done, how well the work is done and how many people are needed to do it. For example, if you have a section which is spread across a variety of different buildings you are going to need more staff than if you are all together, but there may be important aspects of the service which require you to be spread out. Managing the service and the people will affect the number of people required. If the service is driven by the number of people available it is rather like having the tail wag the dog, but equally it makes some sense to ensure that the most economical use is made of staff whilst maintaining the quality of the service.

Here are some examples of the need for planning staff use from a Healthcare Trust with which I was associated:

- The use of theatres and the need to get a precise costing of them. Some consultants were overrunning their time in the theatres and the question was who should pay for the overtime of the porters and nurses? One way round this has been to get consultants to manage their lists by having whole days rather than half days in the theatre.

- The maternity unit was getting regional manpower figures on the future number of midwives needed and the number of projected deliveries. The question was how typical was the trust's catchment area compared with these regional figures?

- One directorate was looking at the workload activities of the staff and the dependency of individual patients – the higher the dependency of patients, the more staff are needed to look after them. This was to enable them to forward plan what sorts of staff they needed and how many.

- Another directorate was obtaining information on waiting lists so they could draw up plans for various initiatives such as operating at weekends and evenings. This had obvious implications for staffing and who was to pay for it.

- Looking at the case mix, including care profiles, allowed one group to manage their resources better. By having different mixes of routine and difficult cases the specialist technical staff required for the assessment stage could be better used.

Managing temporary contract staff

A particular aspect of managing flexible working hours is planning for temporary or contract staff. Nursing particularly has always used 'bank' staff to cover for absent colleagues, but increasingly organisations at all levels are using periphery workers to manage the ebb and flow of work and income. Temporary, part-time and contract staff – or periphery staff – need a different sort of managing from full-time permanent staff – or core staff.

- Core staff are full-time, permanent, career staff mainly in managerial, professional and skilled technical positions. They are offered relatively secure employment with an expectation of training and development and career moves when appropriate.

- Periphery staff are part-time and/or temporary staff employed on a contract basis. They have fewer opportunities for training and promotions within the organisation. Some services have become entirely periphery as they are contracted out.

The benefits to the organisation of employing periphery staff include improved flexibility and productivity, reduced employment costs, increased resources for core tasks where contracting out is used and enhanced job security for core employees. Contracting can also be attractive to individuals such as professionals with high earning capacity and scarce skills and convenient for some others such as parents of school-age children. However, the great majority of people seek the security of core employment. There are a number of disadvantages in the widespread use of contract staff:

- Cost – the short-term gains may be offset against longer term costs if the contractors are employed at premium rates for a long time.

- Quality and reliability – it is more difficult to monitor work and the safety standards of contract staff.

- Employee relations – the contract staff may upset agreements with trade unions and with core staff about terms and conditions.

There are some particular management issues associated with managing periphery staff:

- There is a greater need for clear instructions and procedures if things are to be done consistently. This is better done as specifying 'the what' that is required rather than 'the how' as the confidence and contribution of people is better where they feel as if they have some say in the how of what they do.

- Whole jobs are better then bits and pieces. Give the temporary or part-time members of staff something to complete rather than merely assist with, no matter how tempting it is to get them to do all the little things that no one else has got around to doing. This will ensure a more committed contribution.

- Periphery staff are nearly always more detached emotionally from the organisation than core staff. As a result, they are willing to fit in with your requirements. Many do not want to be more involved.

- You need to ensure that periphery staff have access to all the housekeeping information such as when breaks are taken, where lavatories are and what dress standards are, as well as health and safety information and discipline procedures.

- No matter how rare and mysterious the skills brought in on the periphery those in the core must have sufficient expertise to specify and manage the contribution otherwise the tail will begin to wag the dog as happened in some of the uses of management consultants and early uses of computer staff.

- There is a need to recognise that the core staff are involved in helping the periphery staff and this can mean extra work for them.

- If senior staff devote all their time to the periphery workers, core staff can feel ignored and aggrieved.

- Many of the periphery people will work for more than one organisation at any one time and can be a useful source of opinions on the reputation of a particular unit. They can also be your best, or worst, PR department!

> How do you ensure periphery staff know what to do? Do you give them enough support to make them feel welcome? Who looks after their queries? Which of the following do you include part-timers and temporary staff in – meetings; staff development; appraisal procedures; coffee clubs; staff outings; the Christmas do? When do you use external consultants? Do you do it to save time or to take advantage of their expertise? How do you monitor what external experts are doing? How do you control external consultants?

AND FINALLY...

What would you recommend Janice's boss to think about based on the material in this chapter? I would suggest her boss systematically considers the work of the section and sees this as an opportunity to redistribute the work. There may be opportunities for enhancing some other people's work to give them more satisfaction as well as conceding to Janice's request for part-time work. By allowing Janice to go part-time her boss is also giving the message to everyone that home matters. However, there will be implications for her co-workers and it is important they do not feel put upon.

FURTHER READING

STREDWICK J *and* ELLIS S (1998) Flexible Working Practices. London, IPD. This is a substantial book with many examples about this topic. You will also find material in most personnel and HRM books.

6 The management of work-related stress

OBJECTIVES

When you have finished reading this chapter you should be able to:

- understand and explain the causes, symptoms, prevention and treatment of work-related stress in your organisation

- understand some of the issues associated with using the term stress.

TRISH'S CONCERN WITH STAFF MORALE

Trish is head of department in a further education college. She has 10 full-time members of the teaching staff and seven part-timers. Whenever more than two are gathered, they all say how stressed they are. The talk is of how much work they all have to do and the constant demands from the various agencies with which they come into contact. Moaning about the hours and pay are endemic. What should Trish do?

Remind them that they are relatively well paid, on national pay scales, compared with the surrounding area? Remind them that they have longer holidays than most? Ask colleagues in other departments what they think? Analyse whether their moans affect the work of the individuals? Consider whether it is just a habit that has grown up? Investigate whether there are particular individuals who are having a bad time? Talk to senior management about the problem of morale? Look for symptoms? Change the way work is done or allocated? Organise for a stress counsellor to be available?

These feelings of being stressed are not just typical of teachers. The 1990s is wedded to the notion of constant, everyday, barely tolerable stress. Anti-depressants outsell all other types of prescription drugs, and lists of bestsellers include soothing volumes on how to deal with stress. Stress is frequently described as an epidemic of modern times. A few decades ago it was unknown. The word in its current form has only been used for the last 30 years. Stress is blamed for physical and mental illness as well as costing industry millions in lost work time. So what is stress?

This chapter tries to answer the question 'How can we help staff to keep things going when all around things are different?' People at work are often good at looking after the well-being of their customers and clients, but looking after the well-being of the staff is often left to others or not done at all. Usually the argument is something like: 'Well, we must put the customers first.' If we are looking for a sustained period of effort from ourselves and others, we cannot expect it unless we ensure that staff are well. All of us can keep working like crazy for a few weeks, or indeed a few months in crisis, but this is not sustainable over a period of years – we will burn out. If we are investing in expensive selection and training of staff it is absurd to then risk losing them because they are too exhausted or worn down to do their best work. Sustaining staff is a line-management role.

WHAT IS THE ROLE OF THE MANAGER IN SUPPORTING STAFF?

The current thinking about the role of managers talks about the need to combine traditional skills – such as analytical thinking and a sound financial approach – with the ability to listen well, give useful feedback and serve as coach and mentor to staff in order to enhance their satisfaction with and performance in the job. By implication all that needs to be done is that accountability systems have to be developed to support managers, standards set, training arranged, feedback on achievements given and individual assessment and possible rewards given. In this approach there is emphasis on the use of a human resource management approach more systematically to deploy and pay the workforce whose performance determines the success of the organisation. For example, the Royal Bank of Scotland (Rick 1996) has established a framework for all human resource policies and practices with the idea of creating a high performing and capable organisation. The Royal Bank of Scotland model includes the following, some aspects of which are discussed in this book in more detail:

- job and organisation design

- selecting for success, using a competency-based approach

- continuously managing performance, using appraisal and coaching as a key responsibility for all managers and supervisors

- developing individual capability with individually agreed development plans

- business and resource planning

- rewarding performance with clear performance standards and rewards.

The idea behind these trends in management is to improve standards. No doubt they can all be very useful and can enhance the effectiveness of any organisation. Unfortunately they have been used in a cost-cutting environment in many organisations, and so are seen negatively by some for whom 'best practice' is interpreted as meaning 'most competitive' rather than anything else. Another irony is that these newer approaches usually mean devolving responsibilities for people to line managers at a time when substantial numbers of these very same managers are facing being made redundant. I would argue that these negative associations of some of the newer ways of managing largely derive from the environment in which they have been introduced. The techniques themselves can in reality be about improving the organisation of work for all of us.

If line managers are seen as responsible for the management of the people in their teams, they are also responsible for ensuring that the work they are asking people to do is not going to harm them and that the work is sustainable. If they do not do this, their staff will feel stressed.

COPING WITH STRESS

The word stress is very widely used these days and has come to mean a variety of things so some definitions are required. Stress can refer to a stimulus applied to someone, for example: 'The manager was putting a great deal of stress on the new salesperson and she resented it.' Stress can refer to the individual's response, for example: 'The GP felt very stressed because of the number of patients who had been discharged early from hospital.' Stress can also be applied to the transaction between individual and environment, for example: 'Working in the offices that faced onto the main interchange for the city's road system meant they felt stressed.'

There can be good and bad stress, over- and under-stress. When people talk about being stressed, they usually are referring to being over-stressed with bad stress. The consequences of too much of this sort of stress are in the long term damaging to health and well-being. Research, – for example, Mestel (1994) – suggests that there is a link between the brain and the immune system, which means that chronic stress from work or insomnia are often bad for us as the activity of the immune cells goes up or down according to our different moods. If this is so no wonder some illness is explained by the stress experienced by individuals.

Symptoms of stress in the bad sense include:

- short temper and impatience

- emotional outbursts

- lack of attention to duties

- decreased productivity

- increase in number of accidents

- increased absenteeism, lateness and turnover of staff.

Symptom

In varying degrees of seriousness all these should set alarm bells ringing that things in the work place may not be running smoothly – some investigation of the problem would be useful.

So what are the identifiable stressors at work and what can be done about it? The overwhelming conclusions of behavioural studies of stress are that it is experienced in all occupations, especially manual work, and particularly where there is routine repetitiveness and lack of autonomy – see Cooper and Earnshaw (1996). This lack of control over what we do and how we do it appears to be the most stressful experience. Perhaps this is one reason why so many people in work are claiming to be more stressed now as they feel more controlled by financial considerations. Individual members of professional staff feel as if they have less personal autonomy than previously, as managers have become more powerful.

Other areas in which to look for stressors include:

- in the work environment – for example, a culture of never saying you are overworked

- internally – for example, being nervous all the time

- interpersonal relationships – for example, thinking other people are not trustworthy

- communication – for example, always insinuating and never getting round to saying anything clearly

- workload – for example, five shifts can be more stressful than four shifts even if the hours are the same, because there is less time 'off work'

- noise and physical conditions – for example, it is exhausting to work close to noisy machinery or in over- or underheated conditions, and this is especially stressful if precise judgements are being made.

Intensive care units often have a high turnover of staff, which is associated with stressors such as grief, anxiety, guilt, exhaustion, overcommitment and overstimulation.

There are various strategies for trying to cope with the stress, aside from the longer-term need to reduce the pressure. The main responses tend to be:

- emotional or mental – crying, drinking alcohol, praying

- physical – dieting, exercise, meditation or other relaxation techniques

- retreat into hobbies, distractions or holidays

- reliance on problem-solving – confrontation, assertion, action-planning

- reliance on personal and social support from family, friends and colleagues.

It is up to individuals to choose the strategy that suits them best and there are well-established self-help groups in most localities. If we are going to help our staff cope with their stress we clearly also need to cope with our own stress by using some of the above strategies.

Merely attempting to calm down everyone who is feeling stressed is not a suitable strategy in the long term as it does not deal with the underlying cause of the problem. Indeed it can be counterproductive, as it often encourages a passive response in the individual and a learned helplessness that acts as a sort of anaesthetic; people become less likely to help themselves. Stress should be seen as an alarm not the problem. Working out that you are worried about tomorrow's presentation, your sick cat and when you are going to make that difficult phone call gives you some strategies for sorting things out and is better than merely saying: 'I am feeling stressed, I had better light a candle and have a warm bath.' Pleasant though the latter might be, they will not address the underlying problems of feeling stressed. As Angela Patmore pointed out in the *Independent* (24 May 1998, p26) the argument that we are more stressed in the 1990s because of a few phone calls is insulting to our predecessors who lived through periods of famine or war. Surely we are not that vulnerable. So what are we to do about managing work-related stress?

> What are the main causes of stress in your department? Does everyone have something to call their own in their job? Is there someone people can talk to in your department, either formally or informally, when they are feeling overwhelmed? Do you encourage staff to develop life outside of work? Do you give them enough time to do so? What about yourself?

HANDLING CHANGE

Changes in organisation and in technical aspects of work have meant that most people experience change in their working practice. To some these changes mean excitement and the thrill of being part of the action. For others they feel like a threatening dismantling of the stable order of things. Although there is actually less change generally in society and industry in Britain now than at the end of the nineteenth century, we all feel as if change is an everyday part of our lives. There are several different kinds of change which can be put into four broad types of change experience:

- *imposition*, where the initiative comes from someone else and we have to alter our ways of doing things to comply with outside requirements. This undermines our sense of being able to handle things and we worry about the implications. New rules and laws are the obvious examples.

- *adaptation*, where we have to change our behaviour or attitudes at the behest of others. This can be very difficult and leads to people leaving or retiring. Examples are changes in attitudes about race, gender and taking on a business orientation rather than a public service one.

- *growth*, where we are responding to opportunities for developing competence, poise and achievement. Examples would be acting up or job changes.

- *creativity*, where we are the instigator and in control of the process. Examples would be introducing new standards at work, developing a new technique or trying something to see whether it will work.

Most of us resist the first, are uncertain about the second, are delighted with the third and excited by the fourth kind of change. As a line manager you will undoubtedly experience all of these and have to sustain your staff through periods of such change. How can you help?

> In the last year, which sorts of change have you experienced at work? Can you think of someone who responds well to change? What about someone who responds badly to change? What characteristics would you say describes each of them?

Managing change

As well as helping people cope with change we also have to manage change at work. The normal sequence for managing change goes something like this:

- establish the project – what are we going to do?

- set goals – what should be done by when?

- identify a solution – how are we going to get there?

- prepare for implementing – what resources do we need?

- implement the project – how do we influence people and deal with the unexpected?

- review progress – how are we doing?

- maintain the project – are there any problems?

This sort of list is useful as a checklist to prepare for change but the important point is that ownership of a project by the staff builds and develops over time. It comes through working to improve something. It makes sense to give a firm push at the beginning of a project to ensure that you really get started. Don't do so much planning that you never get on to the action! It is also important to offer plenty of help and support to your staff – and this help is better done after the initial planning. There is plenty of advice about how to manage change – see, for example, McCalman and Paton (1992) – and it is not my intention to deal in any detail with introducing change here. However, there are some useful questions to ask about managing people involved in change.

There are several questions you need to ask when trying to persuade people to change. These include the following:

- What is in it for them? If people can see that the new behaviour, procedure or technology will make their work more satisfying, they are likely to be enthusiastic. If they cannot see any benefit they are likely to be resistant.

- Have they had a say in the change? If people help to create a new scheme they are more committed to trying to make it work. This needs to be a genuine opportunity to participate in the introduction, design, execution and feedback of the new programme. If people are not involved at all, or the consultation is a sham, then their innovative and creative behaviours will often be used to demonstrate just why something will not work.

• Is it clear what change is envisaged? We need a clear vision of what we are trying to achieve if we are to persuade others to become involved. It needs to be put into terms that others will understand, because not everyone speaks in management terms!

What changes, large and small, have you experienced at work in the last three months? Which of these were successfully achieved? Does anything distinguish these from the more problematic? When you want to introduce some new aspect to the work of your team, will you try using the questions above?

Keeping something stable in a period of change

For a satisfactory life we all need a balance of novel experiences and experiences that give us comfort or stability. How each of us wishes to balance these will vary, as will the interpretation of novelty and comfort – your comfort may be my novelty. The stimulation of novelty and change usually means we will put effort into something. However, if the stimulation becomes too great we are less able to make a contribution. It is at this point that stress is experienced, with all the associated feelings of increased ambiguity and the possibility of failure.

As long ago as 1970, Toffler recognised that we can cope with a great deal of change, pressure, complexity and confusion if at least one area of our lives is relatively stable. We can rely on this stable part of our lives and so risk change elsewhere. If we have nothing stable, everything becomes turmoil. He suggested that stability zones were all-important to each of us but that each of us had different ones. The main stability zones described by Toffler are:

• ideas – moral, religious, political beliefs

• places – home, town, pub, place of work that we know well

- people – spouse, partner, parents, old friends with whom we share our lives

- organisations – church, employer, clubs that we belong to

- things and habits – possessions we know how to use, routines that we recognise.

We all need at least one of these to be secure. Working out where our stability zones are and maintaining them helps us to cope with stress in other areas.

Schein (1978) developed this idea of stability zones for the work place. He coined the phrase 'career anchors' to suggest that there are distinct categories of stability zone at work and that individuals use them to evaluate themselves. Each of us will have one of these as most important in our working lives:

- managerial competence – seeking out opportunities to manage and take responsibility

- technical competence – enjoying the technical activity of engineering, IT or medicine, for example

- security – job security, income and pension are foremost considerations

- creativity – important for those who want to build something of their own, such as a new process, theory, technique or product

- autonomy and independence – where valuing freedom from constraints and having your own lifestyle is the most important thing about work.

There are various other strategies for keeping one's balance when there is a period of rapid and unsettling change. In addition to the long-term strategy of trying to keep something stable – such as the stability zones or career anchors listed above – there are the smaller strategies, such as trying to calm the pace at which you work by breathing slowly for a second or two. You might also try to remember that you do not have to deal with something on your own. Asking for help can bring new insights, companionship and learning. Even just unloading your fears and frustration can make it easier to cope. But beware the danger of becoming a real advice junkie!

> What are your stability zones? What are those of the people who work for you? What are your career anchors? Have any of the people who work for you got unreasonable career anchors? To whom could you go for advice and succour with problems at work?

MANAGING TIME

One aspect of maintaining staff in periods of high demand is to help them manage their time. It is also helpful to them and yourself if you manage your own time well so as to make as much time available as possible for 'having a chat'. One way to start this is to keep a simple activity diary for a few days listing all the things you do as you go along. Then have a look at it and see how much you are doing to please others and where and when you have a real choice about whether and what to do. Jobs vary enormously in the degree of choice there is about what to do but so do people vary enormously in their interpretation about what is essential.

It is also worth making a list of all the demands that come in to you over a couple of days to see just what decisions could be made about whether and what to do. Most people experience too many demands in their jobs at the moment. This means making choices: some things clearly have to be done and some things can be left. The bulk, in the middle, are important things that need doing but not all of them can be done within the resources available. The normal advice is to prioritise these into 'must dos' and 'hope to dos' with possibly some consultation with one's boss or co-workers. However, it is not always at all clear how one should do this. Frankly, if it is impossible to discriminate between equally important things that need doing and if you cannot do them all you might as well do the interesting ones and leave the others. You cannot do everything. Nowadays most of us are having to choose not to do things that appear to be worth doing, except of course for those who are not given the opportunity of being in work at all. It is learning to let go of some of these that can lead to greater job satisfaction.

Have you actually got more choice about what to do than you think? Have you carried on doing some things through habit even though they are no longer strictly necessary? If so, is there some good reason for doing them – such as because you like doing them? Do you make too many demands on some individuals?

COUNSELLING AND MENTORING STAFF

Working with different people often means guiding them and trying to make them see things in a slightly different way. Sometimes we do this by telling them that this is what needs doing. Sometimes we try to sell the idea to them by demonstrating how much better it would be to do it this new way. A third way is when the outcome is less certain but a problem or potential problem has been identified and we need some sort of joint problem-solving. When we are trying to encourage another to take responsibility for this problem-solving, we may wish to use the counselling method for guiding them.

Counselling is not the same as giving advice. It is part of the manager's art to enable other people to develop their skills and effectiveness by helping them to find solutions to problems and develop strengths of their own. The role of the counsellor is to provide a different perspective from which to try out ideas. Those being counselled need to find their own solutions and exercise their own responsibility. Neither the counsellor nor the counselled knows the 'answer' before the interview begins: it emerges from the process itself.

This process can be effective only if the counsellor is willing to listen. Listening requires more than just allowing the other person to talk. There must be a willingness to believe that the other person has something to say and to make sure that you have understood it. This requires the counsellor to pay attention to the other and not to be distracted. It needs to be clear that there is plenty of time for the discussion, with no furtive glances at the watch. The meeting needs to be private and free from interruption.

The style, warmth, integrity and authority of the counsellor are going to be the key to how effective the process is. There are some sequences for counselling that seem to suit several people – one such sequence is shown in Table 7. Counselling is not just about getting someone to feel better, it is also about getting people to perform better so they can contribute effectively to the work process. By finding a genuine solution to a problem there is a better chance of the solution being permanent.

Counselling services are also offered by some organisations. This may be in-house, with its associated issues of confidentiality, or outsourced to a separate institution, which may send someone to the place of work on a regular basis or when required. Organisations with occupational health departments tend to do it in-house, as the nurse has historically often played this counselling role alongside his or her other duties.

Table 7 **Stages in a counselling interview**

1 *Factual interchange* Focus on the facts of the situation first. Ask factual questions and provide factual information, like the doctor asking about the location of the pain and other symptoms, rather than demonstrating dismay. This provides a basis for later analysis.

2 *Opinion interchange* Open the matter up for discussion by asking for the client's opinions and feelings, but not offering any criticism, nor making any decisions. Gradually, the matter is better understood by both counsellor and client.

3 *Joint problem-solving* Ask the client to analyse the situation described. The client will receive help from the counsellor in questioning and focus, but it must be the client's own analysis, with the counsellor resisting the temptation to produce answers.

4 *Decision-making* The counsellor helps to generate alternative lines of action for the client to consider and they both share in deciding what to do. Only the client can behave differently, but the counsellor may be able to help a change in behaviour by facilitation.

Source: D Torrington *and* J Weightman, *Action Management*, London, Institute of Personnel Management, 1991.

Mentoring is another way of guiding people. Mentoring is a form of coaching that reproduces in a modern organisation the working relationship of skilled worker and apprentice by attaching a new recruit to an established member to induct, guide, coach and develop the recruit to full competence and performance. Mentoring means:

- managing the relationship

- encouraging the protégé

- nurturing the protégé

- teaching the protégé

- offering mutual respect

- responding to the protégé's needs.

When would you use a counselling model to discuss something with a member of staff? Are there other times when it could be used? How would you ensure a reasonable amount of time and privacy? Have you tried mentoring someone?

ENSURING HEALTH AND SAFETY

Through ignorance, carelessness or neglect, an employer can endanger the health of those working in the organisation, as well as that of customers, visitors and local residents. Protecting both the physical and psychological well-being of those whose lives the organisation affects is an important aspect of managing people. There is extensive legislation about health and safety that grows ever more extensive as new inventions, and new finding about old materials, create fresh hazards not covered by existing laws. The basic protection for many years was a series of Factory Acts, which were mainly directed at shielding workers from long hours and unsatisfactory space, ventilation and heating.

A development of the Factory Acts are The Control of Substances Hazardous to Health (COSHH) regulations of 1988, which comprise 19 different regulations and at least four codes of practice. The regulations require employers to:

- assess the risks to employees' health

- identify what precautions are needed to limit these risks

- introduce measures to control or prevent the risks

- ensure that control measures are used

- make sure that the appropriate procedures are followed

- ensure that equipment is regularly maintained

- carry out health surveillance

- inform staff of risks

- training staff to deal with hazards to health.

There is a risk that this system can become very bureaucratic and use up a lot of resources without really concentrating on the actual safety and well-being of the people at work. However, there is a real responsibility for each manager to ensure that all the staff working in their section, whether core or periphery, know of any hazardous substances or procedures.

Many of these protections are now part of the EU's Social Charter on the rights of workers, to which the UK has not signed up but which are being introduced by many multinational companies and so are likely to become the norm for British organisations.

Health and safety legislation can also be used to cover some of the more complex issues of employee health. Walker, a social worker, successfully took his employers, Northumbria County Council, to court. He was given compensation for the stress-related illness he suffered due to the unreasonable pressures at work.

> Have you ensured that all the rotas are within the permitted hours? What are the hazardous substances and their associated procedures in your work? Does everyone know about this, including students and placements?

This chapter has tried to point out that stress is really an alarm bell that things are felt to be wrong. As a line manager, dealing with the underlying problems is better than offering soothing unctions as they are likely to be longer lasting and encourage more independent action from staff. It may be that staff are overworked, with long hours that allow little time and energy for the other parts of their life. The wise employer and manager understands that for sustainable performance life has to be in balance and that requiring too much of employees will lead to burn out. In terms of cost effectiveness the constant cost of recruitment and training new staff to replace 'worn out' employees is difficult to justify, to say nothing of the human cost.

A related topic to this chapter are the chapters on performance management at the end of the book.

AND FINALLY...

What would you do in Trish's position? Would you use any of the ideas in this chapter? I would probably try to get the members of staff together to discuss what is really irritating them and get them to suggest what we could do about them within the obvious limits of our resources. In trying to encourage a joint problem-solving approach, I would be aiming to bring about a more active approach to their moans. If there were specific members of staff who were particularly unhappy I would probably see them separately.

FURTHER READING

My colleague Cary Cooper has made a career out of stress in organisations, so I would recommend his books, such as a 1994 text co-written with Steve Williams, *Creating Healthy Work Organizations*, Chichester, John Wiley.

I would also recommend books by the clinical psychologist Dorothy Rowe, who writes very wisely and readably about various aspects of the human condition from depression to the meaning of money. Try Rowe (1996) *Dorothy Rowe's Guide to Life*, London, Kogan Page.

Part 3

OPTIMISING THE PEOPLE CONTRIBUTION

7 The move from compliance to commitment

OBJECTIVES

By the time you finish reading this chapter you should be able to:

- understand and explain the use of power in organisations

- discuss the factors that influence whether compliance or commitment is sought.

FIONA'S DIFFICULT DECISION

Fiona is 29 and runs the Bath office of a medium-sized PR agency. She has three people working for her in the office. Dave, who is slightly older than Fiona, was recruited three months ago. Fiona finds she has to spell everything out to Dave. He takes no initiatives. When given specific tasks his work is excellent, but Fiona sometimes feels it would be quicker and easier to do it herself rather than tell Dave what to do. Sometimes the Bath office is very busy and Fiona feels she could do with a more committed colleague. What should she do?

Should she wait for him to become more experienced? Assume he lacks confidence and boost him up? Delegate specific tasks and hope he fails, giving her the opportunity of replacing him? Have a serious talk with him about his work? Tell the boss at head office about her difficulties? Carry on giving the detailed job tasks to him?

The difference between compliance and commitment from one's colleagues is easy to distinguish. The dilemma for the manager or team leader is how much to use control or how much to seek participation from team members.

THE CONTROL–PARTICIPATION DILEMMA

A useful model is that of Tannenbaum and Schmidt (1973), who suggest a continuum of behaviour by leaders and those who work for them. The continuum is:

- At one end the leader makes all the decisions and announces them.

- The leader sells the decision.

- The leader presents ideas and invites questions.

- The leader presents tentative decisions subject to change.

- The leader presents problems and asks for suggestions and makes the decision.

- The leader defines the limits and asks the group to make the decision.

- At the other end the leader permits the group to function within limits defined by others.

Variation along this continuum depends on the amount of control that leader has over led. It is also about the level of participation of the led. This has led to the use of four words to define these different sorts of leaders:

- tells

- sells

- consults

- joins.

This brief summary is often used informally in organisations to describe a boss's behaviour. It simply describes the movement from enforced compliance to commitment.

THE PLACE OF POLITICS IN ORGANISATIONS

As we increasingly depend on less formal kinds of influence in organisations it becomes more and more important to understand power and how it is used. Indeed, the very popularity of the phrase 'empowerment' in organisations shows the importance of this – see later in this chapter. Power is a property that exists in any organisation or system; politics is the way that power is put into action. Those who understand the subtleties of power in relationships are better able to get things done than those who are ignorant of them. Or as the political theorist Robert A. Dahl so trenchantly puts it:

> The graveyards of history are strewn with the corpses of reformers who failed utterly to reform anything, of revolutionaries who failed to win power...of anti-revolutionaries who failed to prevent a revolution – men and women who failed not only because of the forces arrayed against them but because the pictures in their minds about power and influence were simplistic and inaccurate.

> Dahl (1970, p15)

Organisations have power as one of their crucial dimensions, and only by understanding how power is distributed and deployed can members get things done. The innovative idea or accurate diagnosis is insufficient without the means for its implementation. The analysis of power is an important part of understanding how groups work and how leadership is exercised.

Dahl is one of the political theorists who help us to an understanding of organisational politics. As he points out, this political behaviour comes from conflicting aims:

> If everyone were perfectly agreed on ends and means, no-one would ever need to change the way of another. Hence no relations of influence or power would arise. Hence no political system would exist. Let one person frustrate another in the pursuit of his goals

and you already have the germ of a political system; conflict and politics are born inseparable twins.

Dahl (1970, p59)

Pfeffer (1981, pp67–8) specifically looked at power in organisations. He suggests that the following elements produce conflict and the use of power in organisations:

- *interdependence* – where what happens to one person affects another, such as in joint activities. My work affects your work.

- *inconsistent goals* – where there are different aims. My aim might conflict with what you are trying to do.

- *technologies* – differences will lead to conflict. For example if you have one IT system and I have another, who should pay to make them compatible? Incidentally this is often an underestimated cost of joint ventures and the amalgamation of organisations.

- *scarcity of resources* – the greater the scarcity compared with demand, the more power and effort will be put into resolving the issue. If we both want to use the piece of equipment we will spend time trying to resolve a suitable rota of use.

All organisations have limited resources for their members, so we compete with each other for promotion and career development. On an everyday level we will be competing for a bigger budget, more space, newer equipment, more staff and a greater say over the direction of organisational policy. This competition causes the nature of political activity to vary according to the state of growth or decline of the organisation. With growth there is more opportunity for individuals than in a stagnant state so the politics is likely to have more winners in a state of growth than in periods of stability or stagnation.

Conflict
The reality of working in organisations is that conflict will appear. Whether this is seen positively or negatively depends on the nature of the conflict and on one's perspective. Those who hold a unitary perspective believe organisations should be an integrated harmonious whole, one happy team. Those who hold a pluralist view believe that conflicts between sub-groups within

an organisation are inevitable and can lead to useful discussion and innovation. Radicals with a Marxist view believe that conflict reflects the difference in power and control between the leaders and the led and the struggle for power and control.

The possible sources of conflict have been summarised by Bryans and Cronin (1983) as:

- differences between organisational and individual goals – for example, seeing priorities differently

- differences between different departments or groups – where they need to co-operate but feel the other group is not pulling its weight

- differences between the formal and the informal – for example, a felt violation of territory which may be formally given or developed over time

- differences between leaders and led – for example, a felt inequality of treatment

- differences between individuals and their job – for example, role conflict

- differences between individuals – for example, when one person is dependent on the other to get their work done and the standard is not felt to be appropriate.

Possible ways in which managers may deal with conflict, depending on the nature of the conflict, are to:

- clarify the goals and reinforce those that are agreed

- renegotiate the use of resources

- clarify the work of individuals by having a serious appraisal, redesigning the job and changing their level of responsibility

- change the nature of relationships to a more co-operative structure using some of the material in this book

- re-examine the formal structures of the organisation to see if they are appropriate, changing them where they are not and reinforcing them where they are. Examples are such things as organisation charts, communication channels, reporting relationships and co-ordinating devices such as meetings.

Serious conflicts in organisations are often the starting point for change and can indicate the need for change. If you experience frequent conflict at work, it is worth having a good hard look to try and analyse why it occurs and what to do about it.

> What conflict have you had recently? Does it happen over the same things, or similar things, each time? Does something need changing? If so, what?

Power and control in organisations

In the past, management was seen as having to control what happened in the organisation, with careful control of the minute detail of each individual worker – see, for example, the early scientific management work of F W Taylor. More recently the management task has taken into account some of the humanistic psychology approaches to encourage staff to take more power and control of the details of their jobs. There is still central management control of budgets and objectives but less control over the how to achieve the desired results. Many theories of organisation structure are also theories about who should control what. Power is the extent of real influence that people have in the organisation.

Etzioni (1975) compared a wide range of complex organisations and classified the nature of relationships within them based on the differences in power and involvement.

Members of organisations differed in the way in which they complied with power:

- coercive power relied on threats, sanctions and force – such as food and comfort

- remunerative power involved manipulating rewards such as wages

- normative power relied on manipulating symbolic rewards such as esteem and prestige.

Members of organisations varied in their degree of commitment and involvement:

- Alienative involvement is when individuals are there against their wishes.

- Calculative involvement is where attachment is because of extrinsic rewards such as cash.

- Moral involvement is where individuals believe in the goals of the organisation.

Etzioni suggested that a particular kind of power usually went with a particular kind of involvement:

- coercive power went with alienative involvement – for example, in prisons

- remunerative power went with calculative involvement – for example, in many businesses and manufacturing

- normative power went with moral involvement – for example, in charities and religious organisations and businesses like the Body Shop.

Etzioni suggested that organisations which had matching power and involvement structures were more effective than those in which they were mismatched. This may account for the difficulty that some organisations have in implementing the current fashion for empowerment and facilitation. They may really be command and control organisations beneath the apparent new management style.

Sources of power available to organisation members

So far we have looked at the large-scale, organisation-wide aspects of power. What about the individual working in an organisation who wants to influence events? There are four main sources of power available to individuals and groups to exercise political influence: position, expertise, personal qualities and political factors. The most obvious is the control of resources. Those who control what others need are in the position of relative power.

The bases of power were described in a classic study by French and Raven (1958) as being:

- reward – being able to give the other what he or she wants

- coercive – forcing them to do it

- referent – having desirable attributes that make people wish to refer to the leader

- legitimate – as opposed to illegitimate in the eyes of the followers

- expert – having an expertise that others want.

They argued that all these depended on the beliefs of the followers, they were interrelated and a leader can operate from a multiple base of power.

Using French and Raven's list as a starting point, the sources of power available to anyone in an organisation are listed in Table 8. Understanding these and using them to change what is decided or done is part of working in an organisation. Power is sometimes felt to be a negative thing in organisations but access to resources and getting things done is after all what you are being paid to do. This does not necessarily mean putting others down but it does mean maximising the power available to you to influence events appropriately. Examples of using one's power to influence things within the organisation are:

- trying to increase the sections allocation of the budget and so keep extra facilities open

- increasing the profile of the department so that the service is used more

- trying to get the security staff to help with unwanted visitors

- attending the meeting and being prepared with clear slides to demonstrate why one action plan is more appropriate than the proposed one.

Trying to understand who has power and how it is used will also enable people to work better in their organisations since there is a constant shift of power as new partnerships develop. For example, joint ventures with other organisations shift the locus of power from the traditional hierarchy to those who can effectively influence the partners and represent the home organisation's strategic agenda. An estate manager can suddenly rise in importance when land is being sold. Similar changes can happen when there is a change from having a central supplies to

Table 8 Sources of power

1 **Position**
Resources Control access to what others need; whether subordinates, peers or superiors. It includes the following: materials, information, rewards, finance, time, staff, promotion, references.
Delegation Whether jobs are pushed down the hierarchy: with rights of veto retained or not.
Gatekeeper Control information, relax or tighten rules, make life difficult or easy depending on loyalty of individuals.

2 **Expertise**
Skill Being an expert. Having a skill others need or desire.
Uncertainty Those who have expertise to deal with a crisis become powerful till it is over.
Indispensable Either through expertise or being an essential part of the administrative process.

3 **Personal qualities**
Motivation Some seek power more enthusiastically than others.
Physical prowess Being bigger or stronger than others... Not overtly used in management except as controller of resources. However, statistically leaders tend to be taller than the led.
Charisma Very rare indeed. Much discussed in early management literature as part of leadership qualities, but usually control of resources can account for claims of charismatic power.
Persuasion skills Bargaining and personal skills that enable one to make the most of one's other powers, such as resources.

4 **Political factors**
Debts Having others under obligation for past favours.
Control of agenda Coalition and other techniques for managing how the issues are, or are not, presented. Being present when important decisions are taken, control of minutes.
Dependence Where one side depends on the other for willing co-operation, the power of removal exists. Strikes or threatening to resign *en bloc* are two examples.

Source: D.P. Torrington and J.B. Weightman, *The Reality of School Management*, Oxford, Blackwell, 1989.

new supplier-customer partnerships. Instead of routine administration the purchasing department has to develop collaborative webs of relationships across the departments to negotiate appropriate supplies from a variety of suppliers.

All members of organisations need to understand the use of power to influence others. It is not just the prerogative of the mighty. With increased responsibility and accountability at the small-team, section and individual level we all need to be able to influence what is going on. This is often summed up in the concept of 'empowerment'. Increasingly in organisations there is talk of empowering individuals to take initiatives and responsibility. Empowering must include providing the resources to carry out an initiative and having the power to say no. Otherwise it can often feel to the staff as if the bosses are just asking them to do more, for less. Those who feel most empowered are those who are confident that they can influence others and have the power to get things done.

> Which of the sources of power in Table 8 have you used? Which others do you think you might use in the future?

EMPOWERMENT

If there is one concept from the human resources field that has become popular with senior managers, it is 'empowerment' – see, for example, Foy (1994). This simple idea means that employees at all levels are responsible for their actions and should be given the authority to make decisions about their own work. This is not just to make people more satisfied with their work but also to enable organisations to respond quickly. The advantages claimed for an empowered workforce are better services, flexibility, speed, cross department links, improved morale and compensation for limited career paths.

Empowerment is about ownership of the problem and the solution. True empowerment means that employees have the discretion to take decisions about what they feel it is appropriate to do at a particular time. This empowerment, presumably, also includes the right to be consulted about the nature of the empowerment proposed and indeed the power to say no to empowerment.

Typical elements of a system likely to ensure the success of an empowered workforce, from a management perspective, include:

- performance evaluations drawn from a variety of sources
- variable rewards, including some group element
- tolerance of errors
- enhanced communication
- generalist managers and staff
- giving yourselves time to develop confidence in each other
- sufficient resources to deliver some of the solutions that are generated.

Empowerment can really only happen where there are sufficient resources to take on any training that is necessary for individuals. Too often empowerment procedures are initiated as a substitute for sufficient resources to get on with the job. It also requires roles to be clearly defined and previous managers to give up some of their power.

It is worth thinking about what is in it for each empowered person. It could include such things as:

- a team bonus
- increased recognition
- security of employment
- the satisfaction of developing new talents.

Very often claims to have empowered the staff fall well short of these ideals. The difficulties with empowerment from the organisation's point of view are a greater potential for chaos, a lack of clarity, breakdown of hierarchical control and demoralisation of those staff who do not want more responsibility. But without there being something in it for the staff they will feel very put upon, the whole initiative will sink in a flurry of accusations about the latest fashion and fad and it will not work. Empowerment should not feel like dumping! As Hyman and Cunningham (1996) found in their research on empowerment in several UK organisations:

empowerment in many cases is little different from earlier prescriptions for job enlargement, or at best job enrichment, where employees can exercise discretion and influence over the execution of their immediate tasks, but the overall parameters within which they operate are in many cases not so flexible.

Leadership is currently a popular phrase in management circles. There have been many studies of leadership behaviour but it is still a confused area – as we shall see in Chapter 10. Some of this confusion is because of the aspects of power, authority and control implicit in the relationship of leader and led. The control-participation dilemma mentioned at the beginning of this chapter shows the interdependence of the leader and the led and the balance of power between them. Compliance or commitment is the result.

VALUING: CONSIDERATION, FEEDBACK, DELEGATION AND PARTICIPATION

If staff are to work so they willingly contribute their efforts and commitment there has to be something in it for them. Clearly the salary and interest of the work are important parts of this. But where extraordinary commitment is given there is usually something more. This may be because the work itself is seen to matter, because of the unusually effective leadership of the manager or because the individual member of staff feels valued.

Most organisations are suffering from innovation overload. This is often happening just when staff morale is lowered because of redundancies and a general levelling of staff differentials. Staff respond to this in different ways. Some withhold commitment – see Scase and Goffee (1989) on how middle managers removed their commitment; some withdraw from extra work; some increase their militancy; some simply bow their heads and resolve to work harder – again – like Boxer the horse in George Orwell's *Animal Farm*.

So what can a line manager or leader do about it? It is not usually possible to reduce the innovation overload. But perhaps there is something that could be done about morale. There are several ways that people can help improve the morale of their team by valuing each other. It is a complex social interaction and has something to do with valuing people as individuals as well as for the jobs they do. Four types of valuing are consideration, feedback, delegation and consultation.

- *Consideration*. People tend to feel a lack of consideration from their colleagues when the organisational culture is one of keeping to oneself rather than one of talking to one's colleagues. Even at the simplest level such things as making eye contact in corridors, saying 'good morning' and smiling can make a difference. Evidence from research we have done in a variety of organisations suggests that most people would welcome more of these small gestures at work (Torrington and Weightman 1989). Lack of consideration may be one of Hertzberg's dissatisfiers – see Chapter 12.

- *Feedback*. All too often the exhausting effort that people put into their jobs seems to lack any perceptible output. People need feedback from their colleagues. This can take the form of a formal performance appraisal dealt with in Chapter 9. It can also be informal, such as taking an interest in what a colleague is doing. It is not hierarchy-bound; a junior saying 'That's great! How do you do it?' can be very pleasing.

- *Delegation*. Members of staff are valued when responsibility is delegated to them, but this involves delegating real responsibility not just giving people jobs to do. Individuals must be trusted to make decisions about what, whether and how to do things, not just given the job of completing tasks. Otherwise they are likely to work to rule and feel like machines. Responsibility cannot be delegated and then taken away without devaluing confidence and future effectiveness.

- *Consultation and participation*. Due to the innovation overload it is difficult to create the conditions in which people will respond to change with enthusiasm. However, if they are to respond with commitment rather than stoical compliance then some sort of participation in at least the 'how' even if not the 'what' will help. Although it takes longer to reach a decision if you involve more people, they are at least committed to trying to make it work if they have been involved in the decision process. Whereas if you do not include people in the decision process it will take much longer to persuade them afterwards and they will often use all their creative powers to prove it cannot be done.

This chapter has looked at some of the political concepts that can be used to analyse behaviour in organisations. Using this sort of analysis alongside the psychology and sociology models gives a fuller picture. It is like using different probes to come up with different evidence. In practice the different models can be used to analyse different problems. For example, if you are having problems with the boss you might use material in Part 1 of this book to understand his or her individuality or material from this chapter to analyse his/her use/abuse of power. The balance of power between the manager and the managed, the leader and the led has a great deal to do with whether people comply with demands or commit themselves to finding better ways of working.

AND FINALLY...

What do you think Fiona should do? Could she use any of the ideas in this chapter? I would probably look at some of the ideas about empowerment and valuing if I were Fiona.

FURTHER READING

Pfeffer J (1981) is a classic discussion of this area. PETER LJ (1969) *The Peter Principle*, New York, Morrow, is a classic humorous take on the subject. The author suggests that people get promoted to the level of incompetence – according to the 'Peter Principle'.

It is also worth looking at the currently fashionable management books to get a flavour of the current thinking. Airport bookshops are good for these.

8 Finding and selecting people

OBJECTIVE

By the time you finish reading this chapter you should be able to understand and explain the basic elements of recruitment and selection.

GITA'S ANNOUNCEMENT

Gita, the reception manager, came into the office on Monday to say she was giving in her notice to leave. She has got a job at a nearby hotel which, although it pays the same salary, fits the weekly hours of work into four day shifts rather than five days. This rota suits Gita rather better, because she is attempting to do a further qualification to improve her basic training and the college-based course runs all day Wednesday and the hotel can guarantee her that day off.

As her immediate boss, what do you think is the appropriate next step? First, do we want to fight to keep her? Usually not, in the public sector, because there is a tradition of individuals' deciding their own career moves. But things are different in other organisations, where some individual negotiating may go on at this point. Second, it is necessary to ensure that all the right procedures for handing in notice are complied with and that a suitable acknowledgement of Gita's service is made. Then comes the task of thinking about whether and how to replace Gita.

This chapter is about what to do when there appears to be a vacancy. This is usually when an existing staff member leaves but it can also be when there are plans for expanding or changing a service. Very few of us ever have the task of selecting a completely new team from scratch. Most of us experience the selection of people as one-off events. Although the personnel department will have tried and tested procedures for dealing with this, there are important aspects of the procedure that involve the person's line manager. Only the line manager can know in detail the work that needs doing. It is also an opportunity to bring in changes if they are required. We all expect to meet the staff who will work with us and certainly an interviewee for a job would expect to meet his or her immediate boss before accepting a job.

IDENTIFYING VACANCIES

The business of replacing or recruiting someone is an opportunity to rethink what we want the person doing the job to do. Do we want the same work or something different? Do we want to split the job into a different combination with other members of staff? Is this an opportunity to move people around? The process of recruiting and selecting someone is also the point at which strategic ideas of restructuring and change can be put into effect. It can mean reducing one aspect of the work and increasing the commitment to other parts of the job. For example a move from servicing existing customers to looking for new ones in a sales team may be easier to implement with a new member of staff specifically recruited for this purpose.

Many organisations have an overall strategy on staffing that whenever someone leaves a post the question is raised by senior staff whether that post really needs refilling. In a climate of cost-cutting and reducing staff numbers the strategic question is often received at the operational level as: 'how can you justify this post, surely you can manage without him or her/with someone less qualified or experienced by reorganising and managing more efficiently.' This can be very aggravating, to say the least, for tired staff who see a colleague leaving.

Once you have decided there is a need for recruitment, how do you get started? The personnel approach to selection is to try to be as systematic as possible and to reduce the costs of doing so as far as possible. Traditionally this has been to look at a systematic description of the tasks required in the job and then to specify the personal attributes of the individual as applied to these tasks. This does rather make the assumption that the work to be done and the individual to do it will not change very much over the years. Some organisations using human resource management have tried to overcome the difficulty of predicting the future requirement for change in the job by looking at the personal attributes of individuals to see whether they have the potential for change and development. This approach makes the assumption that these attributes are measurable and predictable. Like so many aspects of working with people there is no perfect system and each of us will prefer a slightly different model. What I have given here is the tried and tested personnel approach to selection with some of the more frequently used HRM methods. A further review of the issues involved in selection is provided by Iles and Salaman (1995).

Your first task is to work out what you need. This involves specifying the sort of person you might appoint; you should:

- Consider the longer-term aspects of the job, such as future plans for the organisation and section and the distribution of competencies and age within the organisation.

- Decide what work you want doing by reviewing the job description or using a competencies approach. Having a vacancy is a good opportunity for introducing change, so it is worth having a good think at this point rather than rushing in to appoint another Gita, or indeed anything other than another Gita! This involves analysing what you want done in this particular job now and for the foreseeable future. When drawing up the job specification, it is better to put phrases like 'To do ... and to carry out' rather than 'responsibility for...' or 'to assist with ...'. If you use the second two alternatives, you imply that the job does not really stand on its own.

The second step is to draw up a job description. The conventional way of drawing up a job description, well described in ACAS (1994), would be to consider the following points:

- The main purpose of the job – written in one sentence. If you cannot find a main purpose, then the job needs reviewing.

- The main tasks of the job – using active verbs like 'cleaning', 'writing', 'repairing' to describe what is done rather than vague terms such as 'in charge of' or 'deals with'.

- Scope of the job – to indicate the importance of the job. This can be done by describing the value of equipment or materials handled, the degree of precision required and the number of people supervised.

This format, sometimes called job analysis, is well suited to using a competencies approach where the statements lead on to descriptions of the behaviours that the job holder would need to exhibit in order to do the things described.

The third task is to draw up a person specification, which is where the knowledge, skills and abilities of the ideal candidate are described. The simplest method of drawing up this specification is to think in terms of the technical skills and knowledge the job-holder will need to be able to do the things listed in the job description and then to think of the interpersonal, generic competencies he or she will need to be able to function in the job. The important thing is to set an appropriate level for these characteristics for a particular job. Too high a specification may lead to no suitable candidate being found. Too low a specification may underestimate the problems associated with the job being done badly. Two well established classifications exist to help this process: Rodgers' seven-point plan and Munro Fraser's five-fold grading system – see Table 9. For jobs where lists of competencies exist these can be very useful for drawing up a person specification.

Fourthly, you need to make decisions about the terms and conditions associated with the job. In most instances, this will be done in consultation with the personnel department, whose task is to ensure some comparability across departments and institutions.

In a rational, systematic organisation there would be a logical examination of the real needs of the section for the work to be done, perhaps using some of the methods given above. This would be followed by an assessment of how many people there were doing the work and some decision about whether there was a need for further staffing. However, nowadays the whole issue can become more political. Management in all its various guises has so emphasised the need to cut staff numbers that a backlash is developing of defending jobs. Sometimes it is necessary to point out what would not be done if a post were not refilled or retained. As an example, one organisation I visited had a decision at top

Table 9 **Person specifications**

The seven-point plan

1 *Physical make-up*: health, appearance, bearing and speech.
2 *Attainments*: education, qualifications, experience.
3 *General intelligence*: intellectual capacity.
4 *Special aptitudes*: mechanical, manual dexterity, facility in use of words and figures.
5 *Interests*: intellectual, practical, constructional, physically active, social, artistic.
6 *Disposition*: acceptability, influence over others, steadiness, dependability, self-reliance.
7 *Circumstances*: any special demands of the job, such as ability to work unsocial hours, travel abroad etc.

The five-fold grading system

1 *Impact on others*: physical make-up, appearance, speech and manner.
2 *Acquired qualifications*: education, vocational training, work experience.
3 *Innate abilities*: quickness of comprehension and aptitude for learning.
4 *Motivation*: individual goals, consistency and determination in following them up, success rate.
5 *Adjustment*: emotional stability, ability to stand up to stress and ability to get on with people.

Source: Adapted from A. Rodger, *The Seven-Point Plan*, London, National Institute of Industrial Psychology, 1952, and J. Munro Fraser, *Employment interviewing*, London, Macdonald and Evans, 1950.

level that all posts with 'assistant' or 'deputy' in the title would be abolished. This led to all sorts of ingenious retitling and the drawing up of lists of major responsibilities and tasks that would not have been performed if the people in these posts were lost. The most astute operators used the stated aims of the institution as the starting point for their list of tasks that could not be done without the 'assistants' and 'deputies'.

The fifth consideration is of core and periphery issues, such as whether a full-time, permanent core worker is wanted or a part-time, temporary periphery member of staff is to be considered. There are management issues associated with these decisions. Many organisations have become very enthusiastic about employing part-time, temporary or contract staff as it allows the organisation to have the staff at busy periods with the minimum of financial costs. However, there are other costs – the less commitment one makes to a member of staff the less they will make in return. Also a periphery member of staff can require more managing and organising and this burden often falls on those who work alongside the temporary member because they know where things live, who needs what sort of attention and the details of working practice – and also because they are there when the question is asked. So the management of periphery staff is often through default done by the more junior, permanent staff. However, the periphery appointment maintains flexibility over future changes in demand or type of work that may be done.

At the end of this sequence you should have made some decisions about whether to recruit and what sort of job and person you are looking for.

> Do we need an extra person or can we rearrange the work between us? What future plans do we have for this section? What work do we want doing? What sort of person would we need to do this sort of work? Do we want a full-time, permanent person or a part-time, temporary appointment?

RECRUITMENT METHODS

Recruitment is the business of getting sufficient suitable candidates for the job at a reasonable cost. There are various methods of recruiting people, which are listed in Table 10. The best method is the one that produces the most suitable candidate within reasonable cost restraints.

This early stage of the recruitment process involves both the organisation and the individual sending messages to each other so there is a mutual exchange and negotiation (Herriot 1989). We can probably all remember examples of job advertisements that attracted us to apply, and others which were very off putting. The nature of the recruitment literature does influence who applies for the job. It deserves careful attention if we want to attract the right sort of people.

Table 10 **Methods of recruiting candidates**

Internal advertising

Word of mouth

Local schools and colleges

Local newspapers, radio, TV and cinemas

Jobcentres

Trade unions

Commercial employment agencies

National newspapers

Specialist and professional papers

Recruitment consultants

Headhunters

Recruitment fairs

University appointment boards

The officers association

It is worth considering using word of mouth methods of recruitment such as phoning contacts or acquaintances who might know of someone looking to move jobs or return to work. This can often lead to a good fit of personal qualities. It has also been established that people recruited by word of mouth tend to stay longer (Jenkins 1986). However, there is a danger of selection being based on 'like' recruiting 'like' and of your ending up with a department of clones. It can also lead to discriminating against those who are not part of the network – and it may be illegal.

The personnel department usually deals with the administration of recruitment – such things as placing advertisements, sending application forms and job descriptions to potential candidates, receiving the completed forms and answering general telephone enquiries. Line managers need to ensure that the personnel department knows of any specialist recruitment needs for this post, such as the necessity of advertising in a particular trade journal well known for job advertisements. For example, the *New Scientist* carries many vacancies for research assistants and technicians in the laboratories of hospitals and universities. The advantages of the personnel department dealing with the administration is that some sort of consistency between departments can exist, with a corporate approach for differing posts. Personnel, moreover, actually have people to deal with the phone calls and paperwork as part of their jobs – whereas you might find that you were constantly called away from work if you tried to do it yourself.

Do we need anything special doing when recruiting for this post? Do any of us know someone who might be interested and appropriate?

Different ways of carrying out the selection process

Having recruited a group of candidates who are interested in the job, you now have the task of selecting one of them. The complexity and permanence of the job will be reflected in the nature of the selection procedure. For a straightforward job a simple selection interview usually suffices. For more complex jobs, a variety of selection procedures are used – some of which are listed below. The important thing is always to involve the immediate supervisor in the selection procedure to ensure that he or she is committed to welcoming the new worker and that the new worker has the opportunity of assessing whether he or she could work with the supervisor.

Here is a list of some of the most common types of selection procedures, with some of their associated advantages and disadvantages.

Application forms

These provide the basic information needed for an initial trawl prior to short-listing. They can also form the basic starting point of the personnel record. They need to be designed for easy use, with the opportunity for individuals to add additional material where they want. Usually there is a standard organisation-wide form for you to use. Check you are not asking for illegal information, for example marital status, number of children or race.

Assessment centres

This is where a number of short-listed candidates undergo a range of selection procedures, including group exercises. The value lies in the variety of evidence collected; but assessment centres are expensive to run both in time and in money.

Curriculum Vitae or CV

These are similar to application forms, except that the candidates select their own ways of presenting data about themselves and their careers. There are now commercial companies offering help in the presentation of career experience, emphasising the competencies demonstrated at work. There can be real differences between people, but sometimes the only difference is in the quality of presentation in their CVs.

Interviewing

Whenever research is done on selection interviews, they are found to be unreliable – yet most selection processes include an interview. They are an important part of the initiation ritual. It is also important for everyone involved in the decision to gather in one place to see how the decision falls. This aspect of ritual is ignored at one's peril! How can you get the best from an interview?

- Preparation – compare the candidates with the job and person specification. What do you need to ask more about? Prepare some questions; these should concern abilities or experience and be related to the job rather than being personal questions. What questions are the candidates likely to ask? Can you answer them? Look after the housekeeping: make sure you have a quiet room, free from interruption, as well as someone to greet the candidates and give instructions on how to find you.

- Conducting the interview – the key is to strike a balance between formality and friendliness. Describe what is going to happen. Start with easy questions for the candidate to reply to such as what do they do in their current job. The flow of the interview is the interviewer's responsibility. To encourage the flow, use approaches such as 'I was particularly interested in…'; to discourage the flow, use phrases like 'I would prefer if we could move onto…' Eye-contact and nodding will keep them going, looking at your watch or your papers will shut them up. It is worth keeping notes openly during the interview. Towards the end ask the candidate if there is anything he or she would like to know and try to answer any questions that arise. Tell candidates when they are likely to hear the outcome of the process and ensure that someone sorts out travel expenses and provides a tour of the workplace if this has not been done before.

• Immediately afterwards, make notes of your impressions. To what extent do the candidates meet your specification? Have their career patterns shown appropriate development and progress?

Recruitment agencies

These can handle some of the preliminary recruitment and selection process, such as advertisements, application forms and testing. They are often very helpful in recruiting periphery staff, and in specialised fields, such as sales and computing, they are particularly useful as they maintain contacts with individuals over periods of years. However, the final stage of selection should be performed in-house, except for a very temporary post, as the individual does need to 'fit in'.

References

These are frequently used in public-sector employment but are almost unheard of elsewhere. They often tell you more about the writer than the written about. Their main purpose is to confirm judgements and information formed elsewhere. They should only be taken up with the candidates' permission.

Selection testing

These are tests of attainment and performance related to the skills necessary to do the job. It is important that the prescribed test really does test the skills that are needed to do the job and does not discriminate unfairly. The tests need to be selected very carefully as many are out of date. More controversial is the use of psychological tests looking at general intelligence and attitudes. They may be used for young people with no track record but should only be used by trained people.

Chartered Institute of Personnel and Development

Customer Satisfaction Survey

We would be grateful if you could spend a few minutes answering these questions and return the postcard to CIPD. Please use a black pen to answer. **If you would like to receive a free CIPD pen, please include your name and address.** IPD MEMBER Y/N

....

1. Title of book ....

2. Date of purchase: month .... year ....

3. How did you acquire this book?
   ☐Bookshop ☐Mail order ☐Exhibition ☐Gift ☐Bought from Author

4. If ordered by mail, how long did it take to arrive:
   ☐1 week ☐2 weeks ☐more than 2 weeks

5. Name of shop .... Town.. Country............

6. Please grade the following according to their influence on your purchasing decision with 1 as least influential: (please tick)

	1	2	3	4	5
Title					
Publisher					
Author					
Price					
Subject					
Cover					

7. On a scale of 1 to 5 (with 1 as poor & 5 as excellent) please give your impressions of the book in terms of: (please tick)

	1	2	3	4	5
Cover design					
Paper/print quality					
Good value for money					
General level of service					

8. Did you find the book:
   Covers the subject in sufficient depth ☐Yes ☐No
   Useful for your work ☐Yes ☐No

9. Are you using this book to help:
   ☐In your work ☐Personal study ☐Both ☐Other (please state)

Please complete if you are using this as part of a course

10. Name of academic institution...

11. Name of course you are following? ....

12. Did you find this book relevant to the syllabus? ☐Yes ☐No ☐Don't know

Thank you!

To receive regular information about CIPD books and resources call 020 8263 3387.

Any data or information provided to the CIPD for the purposes of membership and other Institute activities will be processed by means of a computer database or otherwise. You may, from time to time, receive business information relevant to your work from the Institute and its other activities. If you do not wish to receive such information please write to the CIPD, giving your full name, address and postcode. The Institute does not make its membership lists available to any outside organisation.

1795/05/00

2 21

BUSINESS REPLY SERVICE
Licence No WD 1019

Publishing Department

Chartered Institute of Personnel and Development

CIPD House

Camp Road

Wimbledon

London

SW19 4BR

How much time and effort can we give to this selection? What are the consequences of a wrong appointment? Who should be involved in the selection procedure? How can we match our findings with our specification?

Selection decision-making

Having generated the written evidence about the candidates and in almost all cases conducted interviews you now need to decide to whom you will offer the post. Some system of comparing the results with your original criteria needs to be set up either formally or informally. The advantage of having a slightly more formal system is that you can defend yourself against claims of discrimination more easily than if you have just said something like 'I really liked her because I think she'll fit in'. This is not to say you should not consider the informal 'feel' about the suitability of a candidate, but you do need to be able to demonstrate to another that your selection decision is reasonable and not just prejudiced. One way of doing so is to draw up a sheet of paper with the main criteria for selection along one side and the names of the candidates across the top and tick when you have evidence that they have the necessary competence. Another is to sort candidates into possibles and probables and then have a good look at the probables.

It is obvious to most people that the selection needs to be done fairly. In addition to the social and legal obligations there are increasing economic and demographic reasons to avoid unfair bias. The areas where discrimination most commonly occur are in job advertisements, recruitment procedures, promotion, training and transfer policies. It is the responsibility of the personnel department to monitor these and they should help with specific problems.

The two most important legal edicts on gender discrimination are the Equal Pay Act 1970 and the Sex Discrimination Act 1975. The Equal Pay Act was designed to stop discrimination in terms and conditions between men and women. Equal pay for equal worth is how it is interpreted. This means the two cases quoted in a legal case have to be working for the same employer, at the same establishment. The Sex Discrimination Act aimed to remove discrimination in non-contractual areas of employment and the indirect discrimination seen in such things as advertising, for example 'those under six foot need not apply'. This means you cannot prefer to promote one gender, or to develop only men or women and there has to be demonstrably equal access to experience. The Race Relations Act 1976 and the Fair Employment (Northern Ireland) Act 1989 follow very similar lines. The Equal Opportunities Commission and the Commission for Racial Equality are specialist organisations that provide help in this area. Your personnel department or local TEC can all help with advice in these areas.

The decision-making in selection happens at three main points: firstly, when drawing up a short list for interview from the initial application forms and CVs; secondly, when testing and interviewing; thirdly, the final selection at the end of the procedure. All three stages need to comply with the anti-discrimination laws and should be fair.

> Are we discriminating unfairly? Are we unintentionally discriminating by the contacts we have? Is what we are doing legal?

MAKING LETTERS OF OFFER AND CONTRACTS OF EMPLOYMENT

Usually the personnel department sends out the formal letters of offer of employment. When this is accepted they will usually deal with all the administration such as the formal contract of employment and such things as health and safety regulations, pay scales, pensions and starting dates. Everyone needs to have a formal contract of employment under Part 1 of the Employment Protection Consolidation Act 1981 amended in the Trade Union Reform and Employment Rights Act 1993. Some people choose to send out more informal stuff about the department with this mailing. However in large establishments this may not be advised as the bureaucracy can get very bogged down. The important thing is to ensure that the selected person knows when, where and to whom to report on starting.

> Who is responsible for administrating the letter of appointment and contract of employment in our place? Do I want to contact the person before they start work?

INITIATING THE NEW MEMBER OF STAFF

The first few days or week of a new job are amazing. Remember the mixture of excitement and terror? This needs to be picked up. There may be a formal induction programme or handover period but there are also informal, housekeeping matters that need attention, particularly in a busy workplace. If this is a person's first job he or she has everything to learn but not very much will be expected. More experienced people will also need support as they have no familiarity with the new workplace and so will not know very simple things about systems and procedures. Make sure someone is named to take them round, introduce them, to answer any questions and to take them on breaks.

Induction is the term used to cover the more formal introduction to the organisation and would usually be organised by the personnel department. It would normally include an introduction to the organisation with a senior member of staff reiterating the main goals of the organisation or department. Aspects of health, safety and conduct would also be covered. Then comes the more specific introduction to the tasks the individual will be doing and how these fit in with other people's work. Depending on the complexity of the task and the number of people involved this induction process can last from an hour to a month. For very senior posts this is often called 'handover' rather than induction.

As well as the induction of the newcomer there is also more informal socialisation, which deals with aspects of coming to belong to the group. It is worth remembering that a great deal of learning that takes place at work takes place in the informal setting of the group where members nudge each other into behaving in particular ways. For example, there will be norms about dress codes that are subtle variations on the formal rules – and these need learning. There will be norms of how to speak to one's colleagues, what sorts of coffee breaks to have and when to go home. All will need learning.

In the Hawthorne experiments already referred to in Chapter 1, group pressures were found to be stronger than financial rewards. The group developed its own pattern of norms that were:

- not to be a rate buster – not to produce at too high a rate compared to others

- not to be a chiseller – not to produce at too low a rate compared to others

- not to be a squealer – not to say anything to supervisors or management that might harm other members of the group

- not to be officious – those with authority, such as inspectors, should not take advantage of their seniority.

If we are expecting a new member of staff, have we thought of the following: What day and time are we expecting him or her? Have we arranged for someone to be free for a suitable length of time to explain things? Who will be the new member of staff's named mentor for the first few weeks?

AND FINALLY...

Would you use the material in this chapter to respond to Gita leaving? If so what? I feel that as this is a very practical chapter most of what is here could very easily address the question of what to do about replacing Gita. I would start at the beginning and work through the chapter till we had decided either not to replace Gita or done so.

FURTHER READING

ACAS (1994) Recruitment and Induction. London, ACAS. Available from ACAS, PO Box 16, Earl Shilton, Leicester LE9 8ZZ. Tel: 01455 852225.

IPD (1996) *IPD guide on recruitment*. London, Institute of Personnel and Development.

These booklets give practical, sensible advice about how to actually do it fairly. Both organisations are set up to encourage a reasonable approach to the contract between individuals and employing organisations.

Video: *It's Your Choice* (1993) Video Arts.

9 Nurturing people

OBJECTIVES

By the time you have finished reading this chapter you should be able to:

- describe how to maximise performance through training and development

- identify training needs and some of the ways in which these might be met.

TOBY'S AMBITION

> Ben is the store manager for a medium-sized branch of a national supermarket. He has five section managers working for him. Toby is in his mid-20s and has been in the store for two years. At the annual appraisal interview Toby said he was wanting to leave because there did not seem to be any prospect of promotion and he was getting rather bored. At the moment there are no immediate prospects for promotion, because the supermarket chain is not expanding. Toby is well thought of, bright and an excellent manager. What would you advise Ben to do about Toby?
>
> Should he try to arrange for him to act up whenever Ben is off duty? Should he arrange for a secondment to head office so Toby can learn some different skills? Is there some specific project that would be worth carrying out? Should Ben accept that Toby's career might be better served by going to one of their competitors? Would it make a difference to your advice if a new supermarket was opening up in the neighbouring town?

Training and developing staff is seen as an important part of managing people at work. However, finding the time and the money to pay for resources can be tricky. So why bother? There seems a wide consensus in Britain that training is a good thing.

It is certainly felt to be at the heart of managing change. The government exhorts us to train through initiatives such as National Vocational Qualifications (NVQs) and Investors in People (IIP). Employers' organisations see training as the way to upgrade the skills of the workforce in order to meet new challenges from overseas. Trade unions see training and development as a way of helping members to keep their jobs. All agree that encouraging staff to undertake training and development is one of the main tasks of managing people. It may be the induction and training of a junior, the development of an experienced member of staff or the 'switching on' of a jaded member of staff to adapt to the changes sweeping through the organisation.

DECIDING WHAT SKILLS TO TRAIN AND DEVELOP

The technical skills associated with doing this training systematically are increasingly described in terms of identifying the competencies required, measuring the competencies of the post-holders, identifying training needs and then developing those competencies which are less well developed. Identifying training needs for the people whom one manages is done in a variety of ways. The most systematic way is to compare the planned needs of the department with the assessed competencies of the people in the department and to attend to the difference between these. Reality, fortunately, is never quite as mechanical as that!

Training needs are commonly identified in the following ways:

- at appraisal sessions when the manager and the individual discuss what training would be appropriate over the next year to help improve and develop the individual's contribution and career prospects

- as a result of changes that the department is taking on which may involve a training and development programme for the whole department

- at the instigation of the individual who wants to improve and develop his or her abilities either for current work or for career purposes

- as part of the systematic progress of induction and initial training of new members of staff

- as part of a recovery programme after the identification of poor performance of an individual or group.

These needs can be for training in skills, knowledge or understanding. Increasingly, they are expressed in competency terms.

Competency is something you can demonstrate – for example, 'change gear whilst driving a car' or 'slice bread'. It is clear when the behaviour is successful. These behaviours in turn can be analysed into smaller steps when the overall competency is difficult to achieve. However, not all necessary work behaviours or competencies are easy to describe and analyse. Many of the most useful behaviours require subtle application and experience to be effective. This means many statements and lists of competencies include knowledge, understanding and personal attributes as well as strictly behavioural descriptions.

Lists of competencies appropriate for a particular job, profession or qualification can be drawn up by analysing and describing the behaviours and associated activities necessary to perform specific aspects of a job. To this list are added the other behaviours that are likely to be required in the foreseeable future. Then appropriate assessment procedures can be devised for individuals to be assessed for selection, qualification, training and development purposes. Training specialists have led the way in the use of these competency lists. Implicit in the whole competency approach is that line managers are really involved in ensuring that the people they manage are given appropriate opportunities to develop their competencies.

With a list of the competencies required in the job and a measure of the competencies of the post-holder made, a comparison between the two is carried out and the areas for development or training needs are identified. Then a programme of development can be agreed for the following period.

How do we identify what training we need in this department? Do we leave it up to individuals to volunteer or is there another method as well? What opportunities for development on the job do we encourage? Are there any others in the department we could use for development purposes? Have we started using a competency approach? Should we?

DECIDING HOW TO TRAIN AND DEVELOP

Having decided what needs training and developing the next question is how to go about it. A lot of the professional literature debates the niceties of different methods: two useful books are Bee and Bee (1994) and Reid and Barrington (1997). Like most management decisions those about training and development have to be made on the basis of resources and opportunities available. There is no point in planning a perfect but impracticable programme. This pragmatism also needs to be applied to what makes sense. There is absolutely no point in sending people off on a long course if there is no prospect of them implementing the newly learnt skills when they come back. Equally there is no point in trying to learn a new technique at work if the necessary equipment does not exist. There is also a cultural aspect to this: in more centralised organisations staff are told what they need to learn and are given training experiences to deliver this, whereas more self-managing organisations will expect the staff to identify their own learning priorities and find the resources available to achieve them.

A choice of methods

Many different methods for training and development do exist and I have included a brief description, in alphabetical order, of some of the more common ways of training and developing people's competencies and some of the associated advantages and disadvantages. This is to help you think of something when faced with finding a training and development opportunity for one of your people.

Acting up

Acting up is doing a more senior job temporarily to cover for absence or vacancy – for example, maternity leave. It gives individuals the opportunity to broaden their experience and skills in positions of greater responsibility. The difficulty can be that returning to the original post after the acting-up period is difficult and this re-entry needs sympathetic managing by the returning senior post holder. An example is a catering manager acting up for a hotel services director whilst he or she is off having a major operation.

Action learning

This involves the linking of a real, structured task and action within the learning process using action learning sets. Action learning sets are groups of people who discuss the problems associated with the task using an identified facilitator. It can be difficult to keep the group on the task as individuals develop, but it is a technique found particularly useful by senior staff who enjoy being part of a group as they can feel very isolated. An actual example was a group of six personnel directors from two regional health authorities who came together to develop a personnel auditing form. The six originally met on a course but continued meeting infrequently with a facilitator over two years to complete the task.

Audio-visual presentations

These include slides, films and video. They are similar to lectures in what they can achieve, but video has an advantage over lectures in that it can be stopped and started as required and also can be taken home to study at leisure.

Examples are the numerous marketing videos promoting new techniques and apparatus. Similarly many journals now present their material on audiotape so you can listen in the car on the way to or from work.

Case studies

This is where a history of some event is given and the trainees are invited to analyse the causes of a problem or to find a solution. This provides an opportunity for a cool look at problems and for the exchange of ideas about possible solutions. However, trainees may not realise that the real world is not quite the same as the training session. An example is the use made of case studies for business development and taking on financial control. This might involve looking at various scenarios for a business or case-studies of individual managers and the decisions they need to make in order to allocate financial resources. Another example is the use of case-study presentations for the clinical development of doctors.

Coaching

This is improving the performance of someone who is already competent rather than establishing competency in the first place. It is usually done on a one-to-one basis, is set in the everyday working situation and is a continuing activity. It involves gently nudging people to improve their performance, to develop their skills and to increase their self-confidence so that they can take more responsibility for their own work and develop their career prospects. Many of the attributes of credibility, dealt with in Chapter 11, are useful for the coach. If the advice is sought it is more likely to be followed. Similarly the personal skills of influencing, also dealt with in Chapter 11, are useful for the coach so that behaviour can be nudged into place.

Most coaching is done by the more senior person but the subordinate position of the person coached is by no means a prerequisite. What is essential is that the coach should have the qualities of expertise, judgement and experience that make it possible for the person coached to follow the guidance.

An example can be found in almost any contact between professionals. Just think of some of the best interactions between lawyers and their juniors.

Delegation

Delegation is not just giving jobs to do – it is giving people the scope, responsibility and authority to do the jobs in their own way. It allows individuals to test their own ideas and to develop understanding and confidence. This is often called empowerment. The more specific the instructions and terms of reference, the less learning will be achieved as a result of the activity. With the assignment delegated, the individuals start to work on their own. The decision about when to seek guidance and discussion on progress from the manager is also in their own hands. An example is the director of estates handing over a portfolio of buildings to a junior who is given the autonomy, and budget, to decide how to maintain the buildings.

Discussion

This is where knowledge, ideas and opinions on a subject are exchanged between trainers and trainer. This is particularly suitable where the application is a matter of opinion, for changing attitudes and finding out how knowledge is going to be applied. The technique requires skill on the part of the trainer, as it can be difficult to keep discussion focused or useful. One actual example was with the staff of an intensive care ward who at the end of a day's training about performance appraisal discussed with the trainer and the senior staff how to go forward with an action plan.

Distance learning

This method involves the individual utilising a range of printed, audio-visual and other teaching materials outside the traditional course environment. It is self learning and requires high levels of personal discipline, and it can be difficult to sustain in isolation. The Open University is probably the best-known example.

Empowerment

See delegation above.

Exercises

This is where the trainees do a particular task, in a particular way, to get a particular result. This is suitable when trainees need practice in following a specific procedure or formula to reach a required objective. The exercise must be realistic. Most of us have had to do exercises to master the latest technology such as PCs, faxes, answerphones and video.

Group dynamics

Using this method, trainees are put in situations where their behaviour is examined. The task given usually requires them to co-operate before they can achieve the goal. Observers collect information on how the trainees go about this and then feed back to the group and the individuals after the task is completed. Trainees learn about the effect they have on others. This may be threatening and anxieties need to be resolved before the end of the session. This sort of developing is very dependent on the quality of the trainer and can be dangerous if entered into too casually. Usually the task is relatively remote from work. The most common examples are outdoor activity centres on leadership for managers.

Job rotation

In job rotation individuals do different jobs within the section or organisation over a period of time. By setting up flexible working patterns within the organisation, individuals can be facilitated to broaden their experience and skills. The disadvantage can be the loss of highly specialised staff and their commitment to ensuring that things are right. One example is the reorganisation of operators on a chemical plant who perform every part of the process – including packing – rather than specialising in particular types of work.

Learning contracts

These are usually agreed between individuals, their bosses and whoever is providing the learning experience. They specify what learning opportunities are expected, when these will occur and what outcomes are expected. The aim is to ensure that everyone agrees and the individual is then expected to monitor his or her own performance against this contract. Contracts can also be used in conjunction with informal learning and to generate learning opportunities at work. An example is the case of second-year psychology students from a university, who had contracts agreed between students, tutors and the placements they were going to for work-experience placements.

Learning opportunities

Many opportunities come up in the normal working environment which can be used to develop oneself or others. Look around and see what already exists before using time-consuming outside opportunities. The difficulty is that these workplace learning opportunities can be missed or that by concentrating on the learning the task is not carried out as efficiently. 'Walking the floor' is a classic way in which managers learn about what are current concerns in their patch; they can also pick up on new ways of working and the relationships that exist in the department. By using these to ensure that individuals learn how to be more effective useful development takes place.

Lectures

A lecture is a talk given without much participation by the trainees. The method is suitable for large audiences where the information to be got over can be worked out precisely in advance.

There is little opportunity for feedback, so some in the audience may not get the point. It requires careful preparation and should never be longer than 40 minutes. A lecture to quality assurance managers about the new European directives at a conference is an obvious example.

On the job

With this method, trainees work in the real environment with support from a skilled person. This gives the trainee real practice and it does not involve expensive new equipment. However, not all skilled people are skilled trainers. The essential ingredients are briefing, feedback and support that help the individual to achieve the objectives in a structured way. An example of on the job training is the case of a new business manager who was in the office for two weeks before the old business manager moved to a new job; this overlap allowed for a smoother handover of procedures and commitments.

Programmed instruction

This can also be called Computer Assisted Learning (CAL). Trainees work at their own pace using a book or computer program which has a series of tasks and tests geared to teaching something systematically. It is suitable for learning logical skills and knowledge. However, it does not allow for discussion with others which may be important where the application is debatable. An example is libraries that have programs on how to use their services; there are also several such programs on how to work out budgets, taxes and business planning.

Projects

This is similar to an exercise but a project allows greater freedom to display initiative and creativity. Projects can allow feedback to be given on a range of personal qualities as well as on technical abilities. They need the full commitment and co-operation of the trainee and specific terms of reference. Many courses for post-experience management students have projects as part of their-studies. These are expected to be work based and practical and usually are an opportunity for doing a more detailed study of something that needs to be done anyway – such as a business plan for a new development within the unit.

Role play

In this training method people are asked to act the role they, or someone else, would play at work. It is particularly used for training for face-to-face situations and is suitable for near real life situations where criticism would be useful. The difficulties are that people can be embarrassed and the usefulness of the exercise is very dependent on the nature of the feedback given. An example is the staff of the intensive care group mentioned above, under 'discussion', who practised interviewing each other using different techniques. They then role-played by conducting a mini appraisal interview about each other's work in the previous week.

Secondments

This involves organising a placement in an alternative department or organisation for the achievement of a specific purpose. It is often used for management and professional development. The individual may of course choose not to come back! A common example in the public sector is the case of mid-ranking managers who go on secondment to a particular similar institution, often abroad, to learn specific techniques and standards – for example, police studying what their colleagues in the USA are doing for three months just before taking up a more senior post in the UK.

Simulations

This training method involves the use of mock-ups of real-life situations and equipment. It gives people experience before they encounter the real thing. It can be used for initial training, updating, keeping in practice or introducing new techniques. The expense of creating a realistic mock-up is really only justified where practising on the real thing is totally impossible or where a mistake would be catastrophic. The increasing sophistication of computer graphics have enabled all sorts of simulations and 'virtual reality' to be created for workplace training and development to take place. An example of computer simulation is a training programme for airline pilots to use a new system before actually flying.

Skill instruction

Here the trainee is told how to perform an action, shown how to do it and then does it under supervision. This is suitable for teaching skills, as long as the task is broken into suitable parts. What is considered suitable parts will vary with the task and the person receiving the training. Breaking things down into small steps is not suitable for all skills as some are better learned as a whole. Any of the mechanical skills would be a good example here, such as learning how to service machines or stripping down air-conditioning units.

Talks

A talk allows participation by the trainees, providing an opportunity for questions to be asked. It is useful for getting over a new way of looking at things which involve abstraction. It is appropriate for up to 20 people. It can only be used where people are willing and able to participate. Where people do not want to participate it becomes a lecture. Examples are when ideas about management or the future are being explored. Management consultants usually report their findings to the board by giving a presentation and then individuals ask questions and test out their understanding of the findings.

> Which of the above would be best suited to short-term, less than six months, training and development? Which would be better suited to longer-term goals? Which of the methods are appropriate for introducing new working practices where everyone needs to do it? Which methods require a degree of self-confidence and motivation? Which methods would you find it easy to resource, and which require major expenditure?

EVALUATING TRAINING

If organisations and people are to spend time, effort and money on training and development it is important to evaluate whether it really has been useful. Validation is the word used to describe the process of seeing whether the training and development has achieved its objectives and evaluation is the process of ascertaining whether the training has affected the performance of the job. It may be that the outward bound leadership course has met all the objectives – validation; but we cannot see any change in performance at work – evaluation. Evaluation is much more difficult because of the problems of deciding, defining and measuring performance or competency. Hamblin (1974) suggest five levels at which evaluation can take place:

- reaction – trainees give their personal view and impressions of the experience

- learning – the amount of learning is measured

- job behaviour – work behaviour is looked at six to nine months later to see if it has changed

- organisation – productivity, time taken to do things, absenteeism, turnover and labour costs are examined to see if there is a difference after the training

- ultimate level – the effect on profitability and growth over a period of years.

At a line management level you probably do not want to get involved in elaborate evaluation of any training you use as the cost effectiveness of doing so would not be justified. However, it is worth having some simple sort of evaluation – if only at the level of asking 'do we think this has been useful' or 'would we do this again'?

Which sort of evaluation do we use? Would it be cost effective to do some more?

ENCOURAGING LIFELONG LEARNING OR LIFETIME PERSONAL DEVELOPMENT

Increasingly organisations, professional bodies and the government are emphasising the need for individuals to develop and learn throughout their lives so they can cope with the rising speed of change. The argument is made that the more learning undertaken, the easier it becomes and the more confident the individual will be in facing new changes and moving from one employer to another now that lifetime employment is rare. This emphasis on lifetime personal development is enshrined in two formal developments.

- Continuous Professional Development (CPD) – many professional bodies, but not all, are emphasising CPD and expect their members to fulfil a minimum training requirement every year to maintain membership. Some of this CPD experience is credit-bearing, leading to further qualifications and higher ranking within the profession.

- Investors in People (IIP) is a government-backed initiative to encourage organisations to train and develop their staff. Where suitable systems of identifying training and development needs and carrying out the required programmes of training and development takes place organisations are entitled to a certificate as 'investors in people'. It has proved popular with organisations both in the private and public sectors.

There is a parallel emphasis on the learning organisation which is able to encourage individuals to take on change and new tasks by a process of continuous learning.

Another aspect of encouraging lifetime personal development is managing individual careers. Managers have to learn to manage talent and this includes developing staff so that they build careers to suit themselves. This is increasingly important if Kanter's (1989) comments about security of employment coming from being employable rather than from being employed by a particular employer are true. All of us need opportunities to develop skills and a reputation. This involves ensuring that people have a variety of opportunities and experiences. As Handy (1989, p104) puts it, managers have to be:

> teacher, counsellor and friend, as much or more than he or she is commander, inspector and judge.

My colleague Valmai Bowden (1997), looking at the careers of bench scientists, has pointed out that this nurturing of people's careers can be compared to parenting. Some managers are very strict and dogmatic – 'do like me'; others are more facilitating and encourage self-direction and assessment. Those who are lucky enough to have good 'parenting' are likely to develop into the confident, learning, self-developing individuals who are likely to have rewarding careers. Those who feel ignored and rejected can become embittered. Maybe this facilitating of people's careers is at the heart of the relationship between managers and the managed in the new empowered climate.

> What ways do I encourage my staff to develop careers appropriate to each of them? Do I expect them to want the same things that I do? Do I encourage learning in all the staff, including the established members?

AND FINALLY...

What would you advise Ben to do? Would you use the material in this chapter to respond to Toby? If so, which part of it?

I feel that since this is a very practical chapter most of what is here could very easily address the question of what to do about Toby. I would probably try some sort of special project or secondment to allow other people in the organisation to see what Toby is made of. If he makes a mark, other managers as well as Ben will then be looking for opportunities for Toby.

FURTHER READING

The Institute of Personnel and Development has a large selection of books about training at work. I would suggest having a look at:

REID MA *and* BARRINGTON H (1999) – this has for a long time been the standard text in this area. It is good, sensible stuff.

HARRISON R (1992) *Employee Development.* London, Institute of Personnel and Development. This is a detailed, well-considered text aimed at students specialising in this area. It covers both theory and practice with plenty of examples.

HACKETT P (1997) *Introduction to Training.* Institute of Personnel and Development. This is probably the most accessible of the three but (as the title implies) has less detail.

10 Leadership

OBJECTIVES

By the time you finish reading this chapter you should be able to:

- distinguish between leadership and management
- understand and explain the various attributes of leadership
- discuss the criteria for effective leadership.

ALI'S LITTLE LOCAL DIFFICULTY

Ali is the IT manager of a medium-sized retail organisation in the UK. The company has taken over several small British companies in the last few years and it is wholly owned by a large American retail organisation. The big American boss comes over to address the whole staff at the UK head office on the plans to integrate all the parts into 'one organisation, one product, one team'. The occasion has something of a religious atmosphere, with messianic messages and grand statements of confidence pouring from the American boss. One of Ali's team falls asleep in the meeting. After the meeting several IT team members are shaken by the lack of attention to the details of exactly how and when the integration of the IT is going to happen. Some feel the big American boss was completely wrong in the facts given to the audience. Integrating the IT is central to the planned development of the single organisation.

What should Ali do? Explain that there is a different culture in American leadership talks? Try to influence the senior managers to be more precise in such talks? Get his own team together to discuss the implications, anxieties and progress for the IT department? Tell the sleeping team member off? Make some jokes about the 'happiness drug' of 'one organisation, one product, one team'? Being a leader is not just about being the boss of the organisation. It is a complex social role.

For any team there are two aspects that need to be considered: content and process. First, is there something for them to do? If so, is it clear what that is, who is going to do it and how? Is there a consensus about what the task is and is it accepted not only by those within the team but those outside who may overlap or need to co-ordinate with the team? The second issue that needs to be considered is how the people within the team work together. Are they complementary and do they aid each other to get the best out of the team? Are there some processes that are hindering the team? Are there some sorts of tasks that the team is better at than others?

To answer these questions about particular groups or teams we often end up asking questions about how the team is managed or led. Questions such as: how much autonomy does the group have? How much do they feel as one about what they are doing? What sorts of pressures are on them to conform? It is these sorts of questions that we will be looking at in this chapter. The currently preferred term in management circles is to talk of a kind of leadership that – it is claimed – is different from management in that it is about enabling others to perform rather than making them perform.

WHAT IS LEADERSHIP?

Leadership is one of the holy grails of management writing and talking. Everyone would like to claim it as a personal attribute but it is very difficult to get any consensus on quite what it means. Although we find it difficult to agree quite what leadership is, it is useful to have some sort of definition. It is usually said to include the ability to get people to do different things from that which they would have done otherwise and to do these different things with some degree of commitment and enthusiasm. Surprisingly, it is quite easy for a manager without any particular skill or personal charm to get people to obey orders at work. However, if we want something more from the performance of duties than a mere minimum contribution then something else is required.

All the early studies that looked for the personality traits that make up a leader failed to find any conclusive evidence – except that leaders on the whole were taller than led! In a review of the evidence, Davies (1972) found the four general traits related to leadership success were:

- intelligence – leaders usually have a slightly higher general intelligence than their followers

- social maturity – leaders have self assurance and self respect. They are mature and able to handle a wide variety of social situations

- achievement drive – leaders have a strong drive to get things done

- human-relations attitudes – leaders know that they rely on other people to get things done and are interested in their members.

This traits model of leadership concentrated on the person leading rather than on the job to be done.

Nowadays you will hear phrases about leadership competencies such as:

- maintain the trust and support of colleagues and team members

- set up collaborative and consultative working arrangements

- provide the environment for people to excel

- nurture individual development

- recognise success

- encourage enthusiasm through teamwork.

None of us would disagree with these as worthy ambitions for leaders; they are what are called 'motherhood terms', in that you cannot really be against either motherhood – or the above phrases. But it is quite difficult to see how exactly a team leader should go about doing it. The two essential tasks of leadership seem to be clarifying the tasks to be done and establishing suitable enthusiasm and expertise in the people to undertake the tasks effectively. However there are, as ever, several different approaches to analysing leadership and we will look at different approaches in the following sections.

Who have I worked for who seemed a good leader? Who have I worked for who was not a good leader? What characteristics distinguished them from each other? Could I use any of these characteristics to lead others more successfully?

The roles of the leader

After the early studies had failed to come up with any useful personality traits or qualities that were associated with leaders, another more pragmatic approach was taken: to look at what functions a leader fulfils for a group. There were various studies that investigated the work done by managers and leaders – see, for example, Mintzberg (1973) and Stewart (1967). This sort of research led to a description of the various roles that leaders could or should fill in organisations.

A useful summary by Krech, Crutchfield and Ballachey (1962) suggests the following possible roles for the leaders:

- co-ordinator – of the various functions and work of others

- planner – to realise the goals of the organisation

- policy maker – to work out how we are going to do things

- expert – in the technology or processes of the organisation

- external group representative – to customers, suppliers and other agencies

- controller of internal relations – between groups and individuals

- controller of rewards and punishments – salaries, promotions, developments and careers

- arbitrator and mediator – where conflict was unresolved

- role model – what is acceptable behaviour in this organisation?

- symbol of the group – embodying the culture of the organisation

- ideologist – having a strong articulated mission

parent figure – who can always cope with the unexpected and take an interest in individuals

• scapegoat – someone to blame for the ills of the organisation.

No one is suggesting that every manager or leader plays all these roles, but they are typical roles filled by leaders within organisations.

Which of the roles in Krech's list do I fill? Is there any conflict between these? Are there any roles I should be filling? Are there any roles I would like to add or subtract?

Styles of leadership

An early influential model of leadership in Britain was Adair (1982). Adair used his model to develop leadership at the Royal Military Academy, Sandhurst, but the methods have been adopted in a wide variety of organisations. He argued that people working in groups have three sets of needs, two of which are shared with all group members, the third being related to each individual. The three are:

• the task to be accomplished together

• maintaining social cohesion of the group

• individual needs of team members.

These three sets of needs are interdependent. If the task fails, there is diminished satisfaction for the individual and the group tends to fall apart. If the group lacks unity this will affect performance. If the individual is discontented then he or she will not give their best performance. These three sets of needs, or leadership functions, can be seen as three overlapping circles – see Figure 3. This emphasises the essential unity of leadership, so that a single action by a leader may have an influence in all three areas.

Figure 3 Adair's three-circle model of leadership

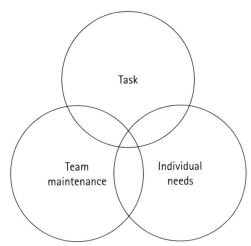

Another well tried device for identifying the leadership style of an individual is Blake and Mouton's (1969) managerial grid. This is used as an exercise in finding one's current leadership style with the hope that it can be modified, at least slightly, to become more appropriate to the situation in which one is working. The managerial grid identifies concern for production and concern for people as the two axes of a grid – see Figure 4.

The result is a grid of different types of leader. For example at the extremes:

- At the lower left hand corner is a 1.1 management style which is the style of managers with a low concern for both people and production, who try to stay out of trouble and simply do what they are told.

- In the upper left hand corner is the 1.9 style of high concern for people but low concern for production. This is the utterly delightful leader, full of charm and consideration who never quite gets round to making anything happen.

- The bottom right corner is the 9.1 person with high concern for production and little concern for people. They are full of ideas on what to get done and what needs doing but are very

Figure 4 The managerial grid

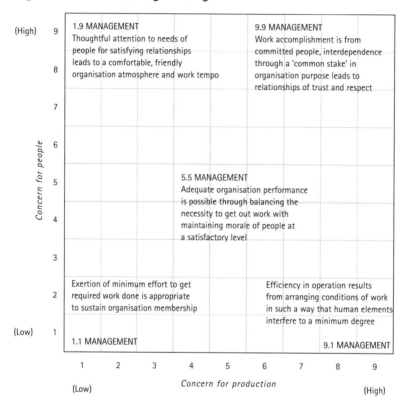

frustrated when no one pays any attention – nor do they get others to co-operate with them.

• The style of 9.9 of high concern with both people and production is the obvious goal.

This emphasis on style, rather than personal characteristics, is probably the secret of the success that grid methods have enjoyed as it provides useful criticism of a kind that most people can live with and hope to modify. This grid could also be used as a way of analysing the general culture or behaviour in organisations and whether the concern for people and tasks is in balance or not and whether some changes are required.

Can you think of different examples of leaders to fit into the Blake and Mouton Grid? Can you use the three circles model as a basis for your work?

Contingency models of leadership

So far we have looked at leadership in various ways but with no consideration of the conditions in which the leader is performing. Clearly to lead in a period of expansion and wealth is quite different from leading in times of hardship and fear. The contingency approach emphasises the importance of the situation in which leader and group find themselves.

Fiedler (1967) was the first to use the phrase 'contingency' in the context of leadership. He argued that any leadership style may be effective depending on the situation, so that the leader has to be adaptive. He also appreciated that it is very difficult for individuals to change their style of leadership as these styles are relatively inflexible: the autocrat will remain autocratic and the free-wheeling laissez-faire advocate will remain free-wheeling. As no single style is appropriate in all situations, effectiveness can either be achieved by changing the leader to fit the situation or by altering the situation to fit the leader.

Three factors will determine the leader's effectiveness:

- leader-member relations – how well is the leader accepted by the other members?

- task structure – are the jobs of the members routine and precise or vague and undefined?

- position power – what formal authority does the leader's position confer?

Fiedler then devised a novel device for measuring leadership style. It was a scale that indicated the degree to which people described favourably or unfavourably their least preferred co-worker (LPC). Those who used relatively favourable terms tended towards permissiveness and a human-relations orientated and considerate style – he called them high LPC. Those who used an unfavourable style tended to be managing and task-controlling and to be less concerned with the human-relations aspects of the job – he called them low LPC.

It is then possible to combine all these elements to show how the style of leadership that is effective varies with the situation in which it is exercised. Table 11 shows the results from Fielder's study of 800 leaders.

Table 11 Leadership performance in different conditions

Condition	Leader–member relations	Task structure	Position power	
1	Good	High	Strong	Low LPC leader more effective
2	Good	High	Weak	Low LPC leader more effective
3	Good	Low	Strong	Low LPC leader more effective
4	Good	Low	Weak	High LPC leader more effective
5	Poor	High	Strong	High LPC leader more effective
6	Poor	High	Weak	Similar effectiveness
7	Poor	Low	Strong	Low LPC leader more effective
8	Poor	Low	Weak	Low LPC leader more effective

Source: Fiedler (1967)

High LPC leaders are likely to be most effective in situations where relations with subordinates are good but task structure is low and position power weak. They do reasonably well when they have poor relationships with the other members but there is high task structure and strong position power. Both of these are moderately favourable combinations of circumstances. Low LPC leaders are more effective at the ends of the spectrum, when they either have a favourable combination or an unfavourable combination of factors in the situation.

The value of Fiedler's work is that it uses effectiveness as its yardstick of success and demonstrates the fallacy of believing that there is a single best way to lead in all situations. It is interesting that the majority of situations he describes appear to call for a generally less attractive type of person as leader, but we should remember that he was examining a range of situations for the purpose of explanation and that situations at the extremes of his continuum may not be very common in organisational life. Not everyone agrees with Fiedler's view that leaders cannot change their style.

THE DRIVE FOR LEADERSHIP IN ORGANISATIONS

In the 1980s there was increasing emphasis on leaders rather than managers. Several people addressed the distinction. Watson (1983) used a well known organisational framework known as the 7-S's – of strategy, structure, systems, style, staff, skills and shared goals. Watson suggested that managers tend to rely on:

- strategy
- structure
- systems.

Leaders, on the other hand, use the softer S's of:

- style
- staff
- skills
- shared goals.

Kotter (1982) made perhaps a more detailed distinction. He saw management as predominantly activity-based, whereas leadership means dealing with people rather than things. Management involved the following:

- Planning and budgeting. This involves target setting, establishing procedures for reaching targets and allocating the resources necessary to meet plans.

- Organising and staffing. This is setting the organisation structure: it means recruiting the right people and giving them incentives.

- Controlling and problem-solving. This means monitoring the results compared with the plan and involves identifying problems and working out solutions.

Everything is concerned with logic, structure, analysis and control and, if well done, it produces predictable results on time.

Leadership, on the other hand, is about:

- creating a sense of direction. This is usually as a result of dissatisfaction with the status quo: it is challenged, and out of this challenge a vision for something different is born.

- communicating the vision. The vision must be the realised or unconscious needs of other people and the leader must work to give it credibility.

- energising, inspiring and motivating. These words encapsulate much of what a leader must be seen to do. People must be kept moving, enthusiasm must be bred and maintained and when the going is tough they must be supported and helped.

If done well, and with passion and commitment, it will produce impetus for change. If no change is necessary, frankly management might be better! Where change is necessary management will be found lacking and the need for leadership will be paramount.

In management circles, human resource management circles in particular, there is presently a great deal of emphasis on developing leadership in those with responsibilities for managing people. They speak of moving from management to leadership. The factor prompting this move is an ideal of moving from compliance to commitment based on the humanistic approach of many working in this field – see Chapter 1 for discussion of this. There is also a feeling that as organisations become less hierarchical and more team- and project-based, individuals will increasingly belong to several teams and will be required to offer their contribution rather than have it demanded of them.

Mobilising this commitment through effective leadership has become one of the buzz words of management at the turn of the millennium. There is a particular emphasis on the visionary constituents of leadership and the ability to inspire others through a suitable statement of the purpose and mission of the group. Words about how people can be taken out of themselves and achieve more than they imagined are often bandied about. It remains to be seen whether this will work and whether criteria for effective leadership behaviour can be distinguished. It is also worth remembering that leaders can only lead as far as followers allow them to – unless some coercion is involved.

A popular distinction between leaders is that made by Burns (1978) and Kuhnert and Lewis (1987), amongst others. They distinguish between transactional and transformational leaders:

- Transactional leaders use styles of communication and techniques to clarify task requirements and ensure that there are appropriate rewards when the task is completed. This is sometimes called 'command and control' type leadership.

- Transformational leaders are those who articulate a mission and create and maintain a positive image in followers and superiors. They are sometimes called visionary leaders.

The latter has become the more accepted definition of what leadership is about.

> What sort of boss do I work for? Is he or she a leader? If so, do I find the leadership appropriate? Is there anything in his or her behaviour I could use?

CRITERIA FOR EFFECTIVE LEADERSHIP

How do we judge who is and who can be effective leaders? Several lists of generic management competencies look very much like leadership competencies. For example the list of the MCI (Management Charter Initiative standards) which is the NVQ body for management, includes such phrases as:

- establish organisational values and culture

- inspire people

- establish integrity and ethics

- communicate sensitively.

These competencies can only be judged by seeing people in action. For many people the only way to do this is to set up some specific exercise, as their working day is remote or confined to specific roles. Outdoor programmes are frequently used as they encourage individuals to cope with unusual situations, especially if there are no designated leaders for the group. In these sorts of activities it is clear whether such issues as communication, delegation and motivation are being tackled. Others use role-playing activities to create similar opportunities to observe and analyse – and usually give feedback to develop skills.

A practical example of this approach to team leadership engendering commitment was the Heathrow Express Construction Project. Lownds (1998) describes how the project managers faced indefinite delays following the collapse of a number of tunnels. They changed the way of working by emphasising that all the different organisations and contractors – including BAA who had commissioned the work – were a single team. They ran development courses for staff on the frontline with an emphasis on 'soft' skills for supervisors, engineers, tunnellers and support staff. These were seen as crucial to the change away from blame and confrontation. The project was soon back on track and in 1997 it won an award from the Institute of Personnel and Development for changing the way the construction industry worked.

AND FINALLY...

What would you do if you were Ali? Would you use any of the material here? If it were me, I would probably use the Adair and Blake and Mouton models to remind me that the task and people orientation need to be in balance. Too much emphasis on either can be seen as absurd by those working in the team. With too much emphasis on the inspirational and people stuff everyone wonders what they are to do. With too little of it, people feel irritated that they are not considered as people.

FURTHER READING

Sir John Harvey-Jones was chairman of ICI and has written several very readable books about management which are really about leading people – for example, *All Together Now* (1995) published by Mandarin.

Van Maurik J (1994) *Discovering the Leader in You*. Maidenhead, McGraw-Hill. This is typical of many current leadership manuals.

Lownds (1998) is a practical example of something that has actually been done – and in the UK.

11 Influence and persuasion

OBJECTIVE

By the time you finish reading this chapter you should be able to understand and explain the exercise of influence and persuasion, particularly for those lacking significant degrees of hierarchical authority.

HANS' THREE SYSTEMS

> Hans is the technical manager for product 'XL' with a large multinational chemical company. He is responsible for co-ordinating technical effort throughout Europe. There are manufacturing plants in Holland, France and Great Britain and a research laboratory in Belgium. It has been decided that all four sites should use the same machinery and methods for testing their materials so that the results are directly comparable. The Dutch have one system and think it terrific, the French have another on which they have just spent a good deal of money, while the Belgian and British sites both have a variety of old machinery which they are happy to replace but can only agree on a third system. What should Hans do?

> Should he ask everyone for their proposals, call a meeting of interested parties, set up a working group with representatives from all sites, decide himself which system to go for and fund the changes from central budgets? He could implement a job rotation for people to try all the different systems hoping a consensus arises. He could tell top management that the change is too costly to be worth doing. He could go on holiday and hope it is all sorted out when he gets back. Influencing and persuading people to do things they would not have done otherwise introduces all sorts of issues about how much to use authority and how much to consult.

At the heart of working in an organisation is the desire to influence others to some decision or behaviour that would not otherwise have taken place. The main question is how can we do this when there are so many different personalities involved? We need to understand how these different people can be understood and influenced. Part of the answer is to be found in the social science models which we explored in Part 1 of this book, which demonstrated that we are complex and that we all have a different point of view which needs to be appreciated if we want to influence each other's behaviours.

There are many reasons for trying to understand the differences between people. Among those we work with we are more likely to put requests, demands, expectations in a way that is appropriate to them. When we are experiencing difficulties in influencing someone it can be helpful to have a range of analytical models to understand his or her behaviour and suggest alternative approaches. When we have a difficult piece of information to give to those we work with we can think of different strategies and decide which is most likely to succeed with the particular individual if we have some sort of understanding of the person. Most of us do this instinctively, the social science models can help to systematise our thoughts and perhaps suggest new approaches when everything else has failed.

Other important aspects of influencing are the questions of power, authority and delegation and the balance between the legitimate demands and claims made by the parties involved. Different organisation cultures will accept differing levels of influence from various members. Questions to ask include:

- What are the formal methods of influence here? This would include meetings, memos, job appraisals, organisation charts, job descriptions etc.

- What are the informal methods of influence here? This would include style of talking, where decisions are really taken rather than where they are rubber stamped, who is 'in' and who 'out' – which is not necessarily the same as the formal hierarchy.

- Who is most influential? What is the basis of this influence? Position, power, expertise, charm, length of service, ownership or just being there?

AUTHORITY

If we are going to be influential having authority will help. Authority is an important concept for managers and is widely used in management literature – for example, Fayol (in Pugh 1971, p103):

Authority is the right to give orders and the power to exact obedience.

Most examples show confusion between authority, legitimate power and gaining compliance. This is hardly surprising as the concept is widely discussed in political theory, suggesting there is difficulty in finding a definition. Carter (1979, p1) says:

> Authority is a concept central to social and political thought, yet its precise nature remains remarkably elusive.

Interpretations of authority inevitably vary with the political persuasion of the writer. Conservative writers will tend to uphold existing forms of authority whereas liberal, socialist and anarchist writers will view authority with varying degrees of distrust, which at its extremes leads to the abandoning of authority altogether and the adoption of an anarchist framework. Here are two anarchic views on authority.

- Guerin (1970) sees authority as tyranny and as incompatible with the natural order and social harmony.

- Wolff (1970) concludes that the legitimising of authority undermines the autonomy of the people.

What do you think?

Power made legitimate by position or expertise is called authority. Without the legitimising of the power in one of these ways the relationship is seen as coercive and unacceptable in societies based on democracy and ideas of personal freedom – see Carter (1979) for a full discussion of this political analysis. Carter suggests that we tend to distinguish two sorts of authority: 'in authority' and 'an authority'. It is an important distinction. The first relies on the position of authority as expressed through organisation charts and job titles – 'in authority' relies on control over resources to influence people. The second sort of authority, 'an authority', is based on personal attributes, credibility or ability to influence people. Being in authority confers the right to control and judge the actions of others. Leadership is the exercise of the power conferred by that right in such a way as to win a willing and positive, rather than a grudging and negative response. Being an authority is often the basis of credibility.

Credibility

Managers are people who are expected to influence people both within and without the organisation. Managers are people with authority, stemming from the position they hold: they are in authority, with all the formal power that the position confers. Successful managers have something more: they are an authority, possessing skill, knowledge and expertise that others consult willingly. Credibility is the word used in organisations, particularly amongst professionals, to describe this prerequisite ability that you need in order to get things done. In the increasingly informal working of organisations this credibility is something you have to earn and maintain for yourself. The job title and organisational position will help but will not be sufficient. Those with high credibility are worthy of belief, trustworthy, convincing and respected. They are listened to and can achieve things willingly and quickly, whereas colleagues who lack credibility meet resistance and have to rely more heavily on the glacial speed of formal mechanisms.

The basis of credibility is usually an appropriate expertise and some contribution of personal qualities such as hard work and enthusiasm. It is a very rare individual who can rely on personal attributes alone to be credible. Leadership is more often made up of hard work, understanding of the position and position power. The components of a leader's credibility might be:

- Keeping in touch with the main task – it is only by keeping in touch with the main task of the organisation as a whole and the section in which the leader is located that new ideas can be based in reality. If they lose touch with their operational expertise they risk losing credibility with their colleagues. Staff can become sceptical about how much they understand current operational problems and the manager will retreat further into management and administration. This in turn creates unnecessary and superfluous systems of control that infuriate the staff.

- Legitimacy – staff on the receiving end of managers exercising authority respond readily only when they perceive the authority to be legitimate. The formal organisation charts, job titles and pay structures provide in authority legitimacy. Western society and its organisations have developed a taste for informal means to supplement these. Keeping in touch with the main task and maintaining technical competence is the main feature but an authority is also legitimised by behaviour such as showing willingness to do things, working hard and demonstrating enthusiasm. Belonging to the organisation and being seen to be committed to it can be crucial in enabling one to influence things. Experience enables some people to develop a 'nose' for appropriate times and actions. They have invaluable legitimacy. The fact that these cannot be learned does not reduce their importance.

- A clear role – we have found that many managerial jobs do not have any clear role. People with these jobs are not in charge of anything and consequently the individuals, who are often hard working, experienced and keen, will find work to do. Not all of this is helpful as it often interferes with other people's work, particularly where the work created is predominantly administrative and increases the amount of administration done by those required to respond. For further details of these components of credibility see a series of studies we made – (Weightman (1986), Torrington and Weightman (1982), (1987) and (1989)).

Behaviour that undermines credibility includes: appearing to do useless things, adding to the burden of others unnecessarily and bandwagoning for personal gain. But different cultures and organisations will reflect different things so any particular organisation may well have other behaviours that add to or subtract from credibility. The important thing is to know what is the basis of your credibility and to work on maintaining it. The consequences of not having credibility are that those working with you will be frustrated and less compliant, peers will take you less seriously, bosses may only include you as a backup to themselves and customers, clients, and others outside the organisation may come to devalue the whole organisation.

Just as important as acquiring credibility is the process of maintaining credibility. It is no use relying on expertise and practical experience that is five or ten years old. No young member of staff will be impressed with 'Well, we used to do it like this and it was fine' or '15 years ago we had the same problem and I managed to fix it.' Far better to offer the advice as current and try to encourage a mutual problem-solving approach.

> Who has real credibility round here? What is the basis of this credibility? What is the basis of my credibility? Is this based on old expertise? What am I doing to maintain my credibility? Is this mostly based on technical expertise or personal qualities? What do I do to maintain my credibility with my staff? What do I do to maintain my credibility with my colleagues elsewhere in the organisation and in other places? What are we doing to ensure that others can build and develop their own credibility? Are we doing anything to undermine their credibility? Can we do something to prevent that?

Delegation

An issue closely related to authority and credibility is that of delegation. When, where and how do individuals delegate? Most books on management will have a chapter on delegation, as in order to manage the work of another some sort of delegation is involved. Usually this means entrusting some degree of authority and responsibility to others. Normally this is perceived to apply more in the relationship of delegating to those lower in the hierarchy but this does not have to be the case. For example we sometimes delegate a colleague to look after a particular part of the project. Most cases of delegation in organisations, however, are from the top down.

Mullins (1996, p570) suggests that delegation is founded on the concepts of:

- authority – the right to make decisions and take actions

- responsibility – the obligation to perform certain duties

- accountability (ultimate responsibility) – cannot be delegated as the senior is ultimately responsible for the acts of the subordinates.

Most textbooks suggest that authority should be equivalent to responsibility. Responsibility without the authority to get things done is utterly frustrating for the people involved.

Advantages of delegation are:

- It contributes to the training and development of people.

- It makes use of time more efficient.

- It makes it easier to perform tasks in diverse geographical locations.

- Expertise and specialisms can be developed and used.

- It is cheaper.

Some disadvantages of delegation are:

- You are dependent on others to perform appropriately.

- You may be afraid of others doing better or worse than you.

- It may not fit organisational culture.

Delegation is not giving people jobs to do, it is giving people scope, responsibility and authority. The question to ask is, can the person try their own ideas, develop understanding and confidence? The more specific the instructions and terms of reference the less learning will be possible as a result of the activity. Chapter 7 has a section on empowerment, which is a form of delegation – see also Chapter 9 on nurturing others in the organisation for further discussion of this and related areas.

NETWORKING

An important aspect of influence and persuasion is knowing people and them knowing us in return. Creating a network of contacts is crucial to getting things done easily. In a useful study of general managers, Kotter (1982) concluded that the work of senior managers could be analysed into the agendas of work that they set themselves and the network of contacts they maintained to implement these agendas. Having a network of contacts both inside and outside the organisation enabled people to consult about new projects effectively. A network also meant that they heard and understood when things began going wrong rather than having to wait until they had gone wrong. People who rely on formal relationships will be told only what they expect to hear and only at arranged times – when they *need* to be told.

Agenda setting is one way in which people impose their will on the situation around them. The other is by setting up and maintaining a network of contacts through which the agendas are implemented. Agendas and networks are interdependent as it is often through contact with people in the network that the agenda is kept up to date and appropriate. Networks are quite different from the formal structures, although there is no substitute for them in large organisations. Networks are made up of a whole range of people both inside and outside the organisation who can help implement the agenda. They are also a source of information about what should be on the agenda. A network is the people who can help things along by speeding things up, providing information, jumping a queue, endorsing a proposal in a meeting, checking data, arranging for you to meet someone with relevant expertise and of course doing jobs. Networks are peopled by people who work for you, people you have worked with in the past, useful experts, people who understand the system and a wide range of personal contacts. Expertise and personal charm are as important as position in the organisation for setting up and maintaining networks. There is usually some reciprocity implied in networks – 'you owe me one' is often heard.

Some will claim that this networking can become too political. How can we judge whether we are becoming too political in our behaviour? A useful test is to distinguish between setting agendas for action and using networks to implement the agendas. Political behaviour is potentially useful when it is deployed to put agendas into action. It is counterproductive when it is deployed only to build and maintain networks.

Too much network and not enough agenda is associated with the type of people who are more concerned with their own promotion and position rather than getting on with the job. The person who underemphasises networks and concentrates on agendas can be inward-looking and fail to take power seriously – and consequently fail to influence events sufficiently. Both these characters can be found in any organisation, but the former is more likely to be in managerial positions. For example, June was the manager in the beauty and haberdashery department of a large department store. She was a friendly, outgoing woman. She willingly went to meetings and conferences and everyone knew her. Her colleagues in the department felt that she never really had any view of what should happen and so always followed the latest fashions and management requests. Perhaps June would have been better advised to use her obvious social skills for networking to inform her views and develop an agenda about the department. Another example is Paul who was the ward manager for the orthopaedic ward. He was passionate about the needs of people in traction and in hospital for relatively long periods of time. However his style was rather brusque and intense, so others tended to avoid him where possible. He might have been advised to learn some of the influencing skills of networking.

Make a list of all the individuals who can affect how effective I am in my work but with whom I do not have a formal working relationship. Is there anyone not on my list who should be? Are there any people on the list who I need better communication with? What am I going to do about it?

NEGOTIATING

A special sort of influencing is the formal procedure of negotiating. This may be the business of negotiating a contract for supplying a service or products. It may be negotiating one's own terms and conditions of employment. It may be negotiating with a neighbouring firm to develop some waste land as a car park for both organisations. The important thing is that in most negotiations both sides expect to gain.

There are different sorts of negotiation problems. When there are just two players it is a situation of mutual dependence. Fifty/ fifty sharing is a natural solution to the problem in these sorts of negotiations because it has an appearance of fairness. Getting there may take some time because of the element of ritual and the need for face-saving in some negotiations, but the fairness principle does seem typical of British organisational behaviour.

Another sort of negotiation is where the number of potential parties on either side increases. Then the numbers and bargaining power of each member matter less. Here it becomes more useful in negotiation if the joint group can create a bigger pool to negotiate about – that is, they try to find more customers, clients or users of the product/service so everyone can have a bit more. For example, when purchaser and supplier are negotiating on a one-to-one basis it is reasonable to bargain about the fifty/fifty split. Whereas if there are several providers and suppliers negotiating together there may be more to be said about trying to generate more business than about exactly how it is split. This is certainly a lesson being taken up by conglomerates of leisure and tourist facilities in some towns who have found themselves a stronger negotiating position by grouping, and marketing the place generally to attract visitors.

Meetings

A particular form of power, authority and influence at work in organisations is the meeting. Many people in large organisations spend a good deal of time attending, and complaining about, meetings. The usual question is 'what is the point of this meeting?' Meetings have both overt and covert reasons for taking place. Some of these reasons are given below.

Overt reasons for meetings:

- Making decisions – the meeting may be the focus of decision-making, with all the appropriate people present to enable the decision to take place or, as often happens, prior discussions have arrived at the decisions and the meeting merely ratifies them.

- Making recommendations – the assembled meeting has to agree what and to whom it wants to recommend. It might also only be a subsidiary meeting to recommend to a more senior meeting where the real decision will take place.

- Training newcomers to the group – it is often through attending meetings that managers learn about the wider implications of the work of their unit and the issues facing the organisation as a whole. Meetings are also a source of learning about the politics and power play within the organisation.

- Analysis and report – organising material for another group. This is particularly the function of working parties.

- Information – exchanging information and asking for information which usually takes place under the 'any other business' or 'matters arising' sections in formal meetings.

Covert reasons for meetings, which on the whole are good reasons although hidden, include:

- Cohesion – feeling part of the whole by chatting beforehand, catching someone's eye or joking. Some regular meetings try to engender this clubbiness by having regular breakfast meetings of the management team or an occasional 'away day' in a hotel.

- Catharsis – sometimes it is useful to give vent to anger even when nothing can be done. At least people feel they 'have had their say'.

- Manipulation – where a particular decision or action is desired and the meeting is manoeuvred into agreeing to this as if it was its own decision. This is usually done by the more senior staff.

We (Torrington and Weightman 1989) developed a checklist to consider the arrangements for regular meetings. It was designed to assist in running them effectively so that the necessary communication and decision-making can take place. The list of questions might also help when a regular meeting feels wrong as usually this means something on this list is not clear or agreed on. There are no right answers it is just a list for you to consider if you are part of a meeting – see Table 12.

Table 12 **A meetings checklist**

Who should attend the meeting?
- a large group to represent wide interests
- a small group to make discussion easier and more productive
- representatives of each layer in the hierarchy
- a variety of personalities to ensure a lively discussion
- only those with expertise in this area.

What is the brief or terms of reference of the meeting?
- Does this meeting have the power to take a decision?
- Can this meeting make a recommendation?
- How wide can the discussion usefully range?
- Has a decision relating to this topic already been made that cannot be changed?
- Are there some conclusions that would be unacceptable? To whom?

What should the agenda be?
- What do we need to consider and in what order?
- Is there too much to cope with?
- Who can include items on the agenda?
- Will matters arising and any other business take up a lot of time?

What about the physical location and arrangements?
- Does everyone know which room and is it the right size?
- Is the furniture arranged so that everyone can see everyone else and give them eye contact?
- Is it appropriate to have coffee served? Has it been arranged?
- Is it noisy, cold, likely to have interruptions?

How can contributors be stimulated and controlled?
- Who has something to say?
- How can I get them to say it?
- How can I keep the long-winded brief?
- When should I nudge the meeting towards a decision/the next item?

Minutes or report of the meeting:
- Who writes these?
- Is it important to describe the discussion and issues or just the list of actions and who is responsible?
- Who gets a copy?
- What will be the effect of the minutes on those who did/did not attend?
- Who are we trying to influence with these minutes and in what way?

(continued overleaf)

Implementation of proposals:
- Who has agreed to do what?
- How can we help each other to get on with it?
- Who else can we involve?
- How can we monitor the implementation?
- Do we need a review date?
- What can I do to get things moving?

Making a case

One specific area of influence and persuasion that is often required in organisations is that of making a presentation or a case for something. This may be reporting the results of a project, making a bid for funding for a project, trying to sell something to a customer or client or trying to persuade a group of people towards a particular outcome. Whatever the purpose there are some basic ground rules for presentations that are summarised in Table 13. It is perhaps worth noting that the same model can be quite helpful for essay writing as well!

This chapter has looked at influencing: at the specific personal attributes of credibility and the specific techniques of such things as meetings. How influential a manager you are will depend to a great extent on the nature of the relationship you have with the person(s) you are trying to influence.

AND FINALLY...

What would you advise Hans to do? What from this chapter might be useful? I would probably start by looking at the basis of his authority and credibility, encourage him to build a suitable network and decide what sort of meeting he wants.

FURTHER READING

This is a chapter where the material comes from such a wide range of understandings that no specific text really exists. On the academic side you could look at the relevant sections in a book on organisational behaviour such as Mullins (1996). This is the standard text in this area. More political is the book by Carter (1979), which I do recommend to those of you with a taste

Table 13 **Making your case**

Preparation

Why are you making this presentation?

What are you going to say?

Who are you saying it to?

Where will you be saying it?

How will you say it?

The structure

Preface	Possibilities
Position	Proposal
Problem	Postscript

The technique

Delivery – beware mumbling, hesitancy, gabbling, catch phrases, poor eye contact, mannerisms and dropping your voice.

Language – use short words and sentences.

Visuals – they aid explanation and persuasion.

Detail – better too little than too much.

Feedback – ask them.

Summary and questions

Look at original objective.

Summarise, recommend, propose next step, thank and ask for questions.

Source: Making Your Case, Video Arts.

for the analytical. Pfeffer (1981) is an excellent academic text that is worth having a look at if you want to go into greater depth.

More fun would be to read some descriptions of how people actually went about influencing others. For this you could look at some of the autobiographies mentioned in Chapter 1 or the Lownds book mentioned in the previous chapter. Case studies and profiles in magazines such as *Management Today* also can have good stories in this area which may include useful insights.

12 Motivation

OBJECTIVE

By the time you finish reading this chapter you should be able to understand and explain the major theories of motivation.

IKBAHL'S FATIGUED CHARITY

Ikbahl was the office manager of the head office of a charity. He was responsible for forty people. These people had a lot of clerical work to do, acknowledging donations from the public and sending out leaflets. Many of these people were idealistic, young people who felt passionately about the cause of the charity. There was a constant turnover of staff. Although recruitment was not a problem, Ikbahl felt too many errors occurred because of inexperienced staff and good people were leaving because they found the reality of the work dull compared with their initial expectations. What should Ikbahl do?

Should he accept the rate of turnover as inevitable? Hope that a recession will make people stay in their jobs longer? Try to vary the work by including some tasks outside the office? Look for ways of getting groups to work together and innovate? Have a suggestion box for a weekly campaign? Have a small fund of time/cash for individual projects to increase fundraising? What would motivate these keen, young idealists to stay longer?

In common parlance we often say things like 'Jo is motivated by money' or 'Jan really enjoys competition.' The assumption is that we can see motivation. The reality is that we can only hypothesise that people are motivated by some particular thing by looking at their behaviour and seeing if there is anything different when the particular 'thing' is involved. Motivation is not something we can feel, smell, hear or see; we can only see the consequences of someone's inner motivation. Motivation is a drive within a person to try to achieve a goal, to meet a want or need.

We use the words motivation, wants, needs and motives freely both at work and elsewhere. We talk of Pat having the motivation to get on. We talk to Jan about wanting promotion. We listen when Chee says he needs the project. We discuss with Jo other people's motives for doing things. All these attributes have to be deduced from their behaviour. We are in reality guessing at what motivates people from the way they behave in different circumstances. There seems little doubt that beyond the very basic needs of food, shelter and safety our wants are culturally determined. For example, in the developed Western cultures we tend to emphasise individuality and achievement whereas in many Eastern cultures there is an emphasis on the family and group achievements and fitting in and being accepted is valued highly. These affect what people are motivated to work for. How stable these culturally determined motivations are, how varied they are and whether they can be influenced is the subject of much academic debate that is really too theoretical for our needs here.

Our task is to examine the motivation of people at work. For managers this understanding is important if they are responsible for ensuring that people work satisfactorily. For individuals the understanding is important if they are to understand their own and other people's behaviour at work. Motivating people at work is not just a case of pressing the right button to switch them on, no matter that some managers feel this is how it should be. Indeed technically managers cannot motivate people as it is an internal state that directs people towards certain goals or objectives. The management task is to ensure that each individual's motivation is engaged by checking that they are willing to work, to a standard, for the rewards offered. It is important to understand this distinction as many managers treat everyone in the same way and try to manipulate people by trying to 'motivate' them. A better way is to try to understand the needs and objectives of those who work for or with you and to arrive at some sort of equitable arrangement that their needs as well as the organisation's needs will be met.

This is sometimes enshrined in the phrase the 'employment, or psychological, contract'. This contract involves a series of expectations between the individual member and the organisation. These expectations are not defined formally and the individual and the organisation may not be conscious of the contract but the relationship is affected by the expectations. This means taking into account individual differences in how people interpret the rewards offered. For example, we will all differ in our interests, attitudes and needs and that will affect how we react to different aspects of the job, such as its degree of autonomy, variety and amount of work to be done. We will also react differently to the work environment of peers and supervision and the organisational climate. We all have different reasons for going to work and we want different things from work. Some of us are looking for totally involving jobs that offer opportunities for responsibility and recognition, for example becoming general managers. Others are looking for a little more money and the freedom to get on with things away from work. We have different attitudes to work.

Understanding the motivation of people at work means admitting that different things will have different values to different people. This suggests that we need to understand that those who work with us may not have the same orientation to work as ourselves. To paraphrase Mills (1956): work may be a mere source of livelihood, or the most significant part of one' inner life; it may be experienced as hard graft, or as an exuberant expression of self, as a bounden duty, or as a development of man's universal nature. Neither love nor hatred of work is inherent in man, or inherent in any given line of work.

An example of the different approaches to work can be seen when some people opt for part-time, temporary or contract work, so-called periphery work. Others opt for permanent, full-time work, so-called core work. This can be an expression of a different set of priorities as well as a response to the available opportunities. Why are people so different?

MASLOW'S MODEL OF MOTIVATION

Psychologists have studied the behaviour of animals and humans to try to find out what things people will work for – what gives pleasure and what inhibits behaviour. There have been very precise and detailed studies of animals learning new skills and of

Figure 5 Maslow's hierarchy of human needs

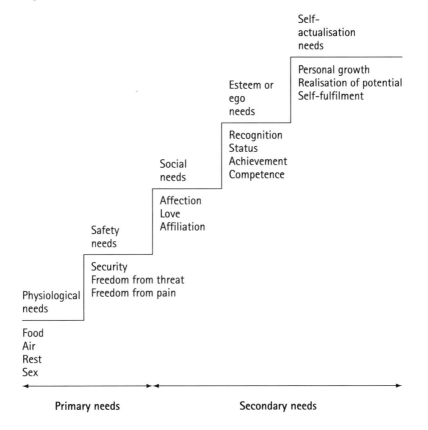

Self-
actualisation
needs

Personal growth
Realisation of potential
Self-fulfilment

Esteem or
ego
needs

Recognition
Status
Achievement
Competence

Social
needs

Affection
Love
Affiliation

Safety
needs

Security
Freedom from threat
Freedom from pain

Physiological
needs

Food
Air
Rest
Sex

Primary needs   Secondary needs

the difference a suitable reward can make. The word 'motivation' is used technically in these studies to describe the hidden, inner drive or need to seek that reward. Different models have been developed to account for the variation in motivation across time with the same person and between different people.

The most famous model of the variation in motivation across time, for the same person and between people is that of Maslow (1954) – see Figure 5. He grouped needs into a hierarchy of five stages. The first two he called primary needs, concerned with our basic physical requirements. The latter three stages he calls secondary needs, which are learned, psychological needs that only come into play when the primary needs are satisfied. They are more culturally determined. For example, if we are hungry or physically exhausted we are less concerned about being free from pain or secure. He also points out that once a primary need is satisfied it loses its potency and is no longer a motivator. In our example, once the hunger or exhaustion is satisfied the person will be less motivated by food and rest and will be more motivated to seek safety. By contrast, Maslow argues, secondary needs continue to motivate and we seek more of them even when we have experienced some satisfaction of this need.

At work, at least in the developed world, most of us have our primary needs satisfied by regular periods of rest and food with sufficient shelter to protect us from the climate. Just think of the fuss we make when the heating or air-conditioning is not working. In analysing the behaviour in Western organisations we are mostly concerned with the motivation based on secondary needs. Many organisations recognise that social contact and belonging to a group can be helpful in getting the work done – especially as relief from a tedious task. In one head office I visited, notices had to go out to 20,000 pensioners. The manager in charge decided that the whole department, including himself, should spend the last half hour of the day, for a week, putting the papers in the envelopes as they sat round a big table. He could of course have hired temporary staff or given it to the most junior staff. He saw the opportunity to get the task done efficiently by bringing everyone together. They certainly all seemed motivated by the social gathering and chattered as they did the task.

Maslow's next level, esteem needs, are met at work through all sorts of status distinctions, for example size of room, company car, having a secretary, use of telephone for overseas calls or not. Many organisations are now trying to reduce these distinctions by having, for example, only one dining room or style of uniform. The aim is usually to reduce the number of spurious symbols of esteem rather than to remove symbols of esteem all together. Not many organisations give everyone the same pay and conditions of employment! Often those in senior positions have more autonomy as to how they organise their time. Not many senior staff are happy to give over complete control of their diaries to the e-mail.

The top of Maslow's hierarchy is self-actualisation. This term is applied to a person who is motivated by the urge for self-fulfilment, that is, trying to become everything they have the potential to become. The idea of self-actualisation has been particularly developed by humanistic psychologists, as mentioned in the introduction. This view has been very influential in work organisations as management consultants, organisation developers and advisors on change have pursued these ideals. There is some individual variation in the degree to which self-actualisation can be a motivator. First, it is a learnt, culturally determined, need. Second, the other needs must be satisfied first.

Maslow's model is a general model of human motivation. How well suited is Maslow's hierarchy in the work situation? Although it was not devised for looking at motivation at work it has become very popular. It is useful as an indicator of individual differences. Its main strength is in listing what might motivate people. Steers and Porter (1991, p35) suggest various organisational factors which could be used to satisfy different needs:

- physiological   pay
                   pleasant work conditions
                   dining facilities

- safety   health and safety well monitored
                   company benefits
                   job security

- social   cohesive work group
                   friendly supervision
                   professional associations

- esteem   social recognition
                   job title
                   high-status job
                   feedback from job itself

- self-actualisation challenging job
                   opportunities for creativity
                   achievement in work
                   advancement in the organisation.

The difficulty with applying a Maslow approach to motivation at work is that many people will not wish to satisfy all their motivations at work. This implies that the motivating factors at work will not be equal for different people, even where they apparently have the same motives.

Alderfer (1972) developed Maslow's theory for work by suggesting that there were three groups of needs:

- existence needs to do with survival

- relatedness needs to do with social belonging

- growth needs to do with individual development.

He called this the ERG theory, and he argued that organisations and their managers need to address all three of these but where growth is not possible at work the other two needs must be addressed more powerfully. He suggested that where growth cannot be met more emphasis on the existence needs through money and strong social actions for relatedness will help to keep people satisfied.

Do we use all the Steers and Porter's list at work? Could we do more?

HERZBERG'S THEORY OF MOTIVATION AT WORK

Herzberg (1968) developed Maslow's model with particular reference to people at work. He described the lower order needs as having the potential to dissatisfy if they are not met but once they are met more of them will not increase motivation. These he called the hygiene factors – if managers do not get them right there will be complaints and people will be demotivated, if they are right no one will comment or notice, just like the effect of hygiene in the kitchen. In contrast to the hygiene factors are the satisfiers. People will work for these and want more of them. These satisfiers tend to be intrinsic to the person. The list of satisfiers are more culturally determined than the hygiene factors, so your group may have slightly different ones than those listed in Table 14. Herzberg's model has been particularly useful in

Table 14 Herzberg's theory of motivation

Hygiene factors	Satisfiers
Company policy and administration	
Supervision	Achievement
Working conditions	Recognition
Salary	Work itself
Relationship with peers	Responsibility
Personal life	Advancement
Relationship with subordinates	Growth
Status	
Security	

Source: F. Hertzberg, 'One more time: how do you motivate employees?' *Harvard Business Review*, January – February 1968.

drawing attention to the way jobs are designed so that jobs are enriched and the quality of life at work can be improved.

> Which of Herzberg's hygiene factors are currently causing a problem for us? What can be done about it?

Some of these findings about motivation can be seen in modern concerns about what makes people contribute their best at work. For example, one survey by Leigh and Brown (1996), using the phrases psychological safety and meaningfulness – similar, although not identical, to Herzberg's hygiene factors and satisfiers – found the following job features are said to make people work hard:

- psychological safety:
  - support – authority and backed by boss
  - role clarity – what is expected and to what standard
  - recognition – praise.
- meaningfulness:
  - self expression – express self
  - contribution – make a difference
  - challenge – feel stretched.

HOW IS BEHAVIOUR DRIVEN BY OUR NEEDS?

The Maslow and Herzberg theories given above are both concerned with what motivates an individual, that is the content of motivation. If we start looking at the process of motivation we find the ways in which behaviour is initiated, directed and maintained are also important areas of study.

A theory which adds an important dimension to the models of Maslow and Herzberg is the *force* field theory of Lewin. Lewin (1952) emphasises that individuals operate in a field of forces that represent subjective perceptions about the environment, the importance of a goal and the psychological distance of the goal. Lewin uses his theory to try to account for the difference of motivation in people at different times. For example, you and I might both want to meet the prime minister. I see the circumstances as far too difficult; the goal of seeing him is not compelling enough to overcome the psychological distance to make any effort to see him worthwhile. You, however, may be in more favourable circumstances or you may want to see him enough to overcome the psychological distance between him and you. As a result, you will be more motivated to meet the prime minister than I am.

An additional view about motivation is called expectancy theory – see, for example, Vroom and Deci (1974). This is the influence on our motivation of our expectancy of the success of our actions. The more likely we think it is that we will be successful the more effort we will put in and vice versa. For example, if I feel that when I go to the library I will find the books and access to computers that I want I am more likely to put the effort into going than if I expect to find all the resources 'out' or 'booked'. My expectancy of success influences my motivation to go to the library. Another concept that Vroom and Deci use is 'valence', which is the degree of preference an individual attaches to a particular outcome. This can be positive, negative or indifferent. The theory then makes the motivation (M) of the individual a combination of expectancy (Ex) plus the valency (V) attached to the outcome, or the equation $M = Ex V$.

One influence on expectancy is the perceived fairness of the results. This is people's feelings about how fairly treated they have been in comparison with others – see Adams (1979) for further discussion. It is based on exchange theory where people expect certain outcomes in exchange for certain contributions. For example if in seminars/tutorials two of us are always contributing to the discussion and have always done the reading when the others have not we may begin to feel very demotivated and begin to make less effort.

MOTIVATION AND WORK BEHAVIOUR

Some people feel that with the increasing use of automation and the advent of computers, the most tedious jobs have disappeared. Consequently motivation at work is no longer an issue for individuals or the managers responsible for organisations. However, even if we accept the premise – which is arguable – our expectations as consumers about standards of service from service industries, the public sector and other organisations make it important that staff are well motivated at work. This is to say nothing of the humanitarian argument that people should be doing something they want to do! Motivation at work remains an important part of analysing the behaviour of people at work so we can improve the work that we do and improve the working life of those employed in organisations.

Understanding what motivates people at work will also suggest appropriate rewards for them in response to their contribution. Although reward management is a study in itself – see Armstrong (1996) – and is the business of personnel departments, some understanding of different rewards can suggest different ways a line manager might approach individuals. They include:

- pay – for time; by results; for merit; performance-related; share ownership; profit-related

- other benefits – pensions; sick pay; insurance schemes and other financial benefits

- work/task – variety of work and skills used; autonomy and involvement

- social/people – interactions with others; recognition and feedback.

In many ways the emphasis of this book on managing people is suggesting a variety of ways of tailoring rewards to individuals.

Steers and Porter (1987, p21) indicate some of the more important variables that influence people's motivation and work – see Table 15. These variables also give us a helpful checklist for looking at some of the reasons for poor performance in organisations. There can be a problem with any one of the variables.

Table 15 Steers and Porter's checklist of influences on motivation at work

---

1 **Individual characteristics**
   Interests
   Attitudes towards
           self
           job
           aspects of the work situation
   Needs such as
           security
           social
           achievement

2 **Job characteristics**
   Types of intrinsic rewards
   Degree of autonomy
   Amount of direct performance feedback
   Degree of variety in tasks
   Work environment characteristics such as
           peers
           supervisor(s)

3 **Organisational actions such as**
   reward practices
   system-wide rewards
   individual rewards
   organisational climate

Source: Steers and Porter (1987)

Attitudes to work

There are several other important questions about work and people's motivation, such as: what is the meaning of work for individuals? Does work have the same importance for us all? Clearly not. Is there some inevitable connection between certain work conditions and experiences and particular attitudes and feelings? What do we mean by job satisfaction? Is it the same for us all?

Most studies in this field have been done on manual labour in manufacturing workplaces. This is partly because this group of people are easy to study, as they have less to hide, and partly because they have been seen as a problem by management. By studying the effect of work and the differing attitudes to work it is hoped that better working practices can be developed for the benefit of the organisation and the workers.

However it is clear that the technology used by workers will constrain the way in which their work can be organised. Whether a work process is done sequentially with everyone adding their little bit or whether each individual can perform the whole task will influence how work is organised. The sheer physical scale of an operation and the noise generated whilst doing it will influence how things are organised. Whether the technology must be in the same place for several years or is constantly on the move will determine how things are organised. All of these in turn will influence the attitude and behaviour of the workers. For example, some technologies like printing allow social groupings at work. Others such as car assembly are much more difficult to organise in social groups at a reasonable cost. Some tasks such as shutting down oil wells are by definition always happening somewhere different from the previous occasion. Workers engaged in these different tasks will have different group attitudes and behaviours on average from groups engaged in the other activities.

The classic study which introduced the concept of 'orientation to work' was that of Goldthorpe, Lockwood, Bechhofer and Platt (1969), who examined the attitude and behaviour of assembly line workers at the Vauxhall car manufacturing plant in Luton. They found that different workers had different wants and expectations of work, that is work had a different meaning for them. They distinguished three main orientations to work:

- An instrumental approach to work meant work is a means to an end outside the work situation. Work is a means of acquiring the income to support a valued way of life.

- A bureaucratic orientation describes people who sought to give services to a company over a long time in return for a career that saw some promotion and increases in salary, security and pay.

- A solidaristic orientation characterised those people who in addition to an economic orientation also valued group loyalty to their mates.

This research work suggests that not everyone is seeking self-actualisation through work – perhaps they are resigned to being unable to do so. It is a useful counterpoint to the assumptions made by Maslow and Herzberg. Discussing the meaning of, and attitude to, work involves our basic assumptions about morals, power, equality, the rights of individuals and so on, all of which have a political aspect to them. This makes research in this area very difficult as different interpretations can be put on the same findings. In addition there is the thorny problem of exactly what do we mean by job satisfaction and the meaning of work? Certainly we need to understand that not everyone is the same.

Alienation

Another important concept that can help explain people's motivation at work is alienation. This concept, used in sociology and elsewhere, was originally formulated by Karl Marx to analyse the effect of capitalism on people. Marx referred to people's detachment, estrangement and loss of control over their lives in capitalist society. Alienation is about the separation of people. It is applied to the way we feel cut off from important decisions, people or outcomes.

The concept can be applied to work organisations. The work we do can feel alien and oppressive. It is thought that it is the way work is organised that leads to this alienation rather than particular work processes. Individuals can also be alienated from other people because the relationships have become calculating, self-interested and untrusting. This is demonstrated when individuals have become so alienated from others that they are able to behave callously towards them without a sense of embarrassment. Examples can be found in some city dealing rooms where the drive to make a profitable deal means ignoring a colleague who is clearly in distress. People can also be alienated from the product of their labours when the end product is not seen or is remote from their control. Alienation can happen when people are not involved in the original decision about what the work should be. The classic example of alienation is seen in large-scale manufacturing, such as car plants (see Beynon 1973), compared with traditional crafts such as pottery where the workers can see the results of their labour and are less likely to be alienated.

People are alienated from their own labour when they are unable to get the satisfactions at work because they are controlled by others and so are meeting someone else's requirements and standards as opposed to their own. An example is when two building societies merge and the workers from one society have to adopt the procedures, standards and requirements of the other. The individual operators can feel alienated.

Marx argued that alienation is an objective state. We may feel dissatisfied with our job but not necessarily alienated. We may feel satisfied with our job but be alienated at the same time as we may be missing out on something much more rewarding. An example can be seen in those managers who have been made redundant and have developed alternative activities which they find more worthwhile than their former employment and wonder why they did not do this earlier. Before redundancy they were in a state of being alienated.

It is an ideal world where everyone is highly motivated and doing exactly what they would choose to do. We may not achieve this ideal but that does not mean not trying to improve things. There are real dangers if the organisation of work does not give sufficient consideration to the needs of the individuals working in the organisation. If work is organised so that we are cut off from important decisions, people and outcomes we can feel the work we do is alien and oppressive – that is, we are alienated. Blauner (1967) argued that alienation consists of four conditions or states – powerlessness, meaninglessness, isolation and self-estrangement:

- Powerlessness comes when people feel controlled by others.

- Meaninglessness is felt when people do not understand the co-ordination or purpose of their work.

- Isolation is where people do not feel they belong.

- Self-estrangement is when people do not feel involved with their own work.

All of these can happen to people at all levels of the organisation and they are particularly likely to be found in periods of reorganisation. It can be very difficult to find ways of reorienting people once they have become alienated. It is therefore worth picking up on the early signs so that something can be done to make people feel more valued. Attempts to pre-empt these elements of alienation found within organisations include trying to empower staff, setting reasonable objectives, valuing staff and engendering commitment. These concepts are all dealt with elsewhere in this book.

> Are people in our organisation showing the signs of being alienated from their work? For example are they demonstrating feelings of loneliness, exclusion, or rejection? Do their actions seem mechanical or uncommitted? Is their behaviour not bound by rules?

This chapter has been about motivation at work. I hope it has persuaded you that this is not just a mechanical process where you press button A and everyone is 'motivated'. However, you can help colleagues to be motivated if you carefully analyse what is in it for them, from their perspective. If you understand what suits and motivates particular people you can design tasks and jobs so that workers are more likely to succeed and feel rewarded. This is surely in the interest of workers, manager and of the organisation you both work for. It also helps managers to manage performance, which is discussed in the last two chapters.

AND FINALLY...

What would you do in Ikbahl's position? Would you use your understanding about motivation and attitudes to work to help? I would probably try to use some of the theories detailed in this chapter to remind myself that there are different satisfactions to be had. I would try to connect the work in the office with the ideals of the charity. Some daily or weekly activity that reinforces the connection might help.

FURTHER READING

Armstrong (1996) is a useful look at the whole area.

MAITLAND I (1995) *Motivating People*. London, IPD. This is a short, practical book.

Steers and Porter (1987) is an academic text with various articles exploring some of the issues associated with understanding motivation and its application to the work environment.

13 Stimulating improved performance

OBJECTIVES

When you have finished reading this you should be able to:

- understand and explain the issues associated with managing performance

- discuss how performance management fits in with the needs of the business as a whole.

HELENA'S JUNIOR

> Helena was a senior barrister in a small firm of lawyers in a provincial city. The firm specialised in criminal work. Its barristers were always busy with referrals and there were piles of paper everywhere. Most of the work was paid for by Legal Aid. Helena was mentor to three of the junior lawyers. She felt that each of them could win more of their cases – particularly Kate who had lost all of her cases. This was not very good for business as solicitors and their clients were trying to ensure that Kate was not allocated to them. What should Helena do?

> Should she examine what was being asked of juniors? Reduce their case loads? Give them more assistance? Hold some training seminars? Look at the reward system? Conduct some individual appraisals? Talk to the other seniors to see if it was a common problem? Go on a management course herself? Discuss it with Kate?

Presumably the performance of each of us at work is supposed to fit in with what everyone else is doing, so that the contributions of each of us makes up the whole. In the past a lot of this fitting things together was assumed and left implicit in the way people fitted into their groups and gradually 'came on board'. Now the process is seen as being in need of more explicit analysis and description with organisations trying to integrate strategy, target-setting, incentives, rewards, appraisal. It is argued that this should focus employee behaviour so that each person adds value to the organisation. Associated with this view is that performance and rewards should be linked. As Kanter (1989, p223) said:

> Can anyone be against the idea that people's pay should reflect their performance? Isn't that how the system is supposed to work?

Compare this view with that held in many British organisations as late as the 1980s, that men should be paid more than women doing the same job, because they have families to support. The aim of this more explicit approach is to improve the performance of individuals and organisations so they are able to compete more effectively in a changing world.

WAYS OF IMPROVING PERFORMANCE

The increased interest in systematic management in the last ten years has led to the development of performance management. A variety of influences made this so: increased competition from other countries and the realisation of their better productivity; the findings of Peters and Waterman's book (1982) on excellence, which had a large influence; and pressure from government bodies such as the training part of the Employment and Education Department.

Hendry, Bradley and Perkins (1997) summed up some of the areas that need considering when looking at performance management generally from a managerial perspective. I have laid them out as a series of questions so you can ask yourself these questions about your own organisation:

- Reasons   Why reappraise rewards?

- Objectives   Goals of the exercise?
                     Critical performance to be rewarded?
                     Contract with employees?
                     Performance system to do what – attract, motivate, retain, control?

- External   What stage of the business cycle are we in?

                      National culture?

- Internal   Assumptions about our work and relationships?

                      Groups and their performance and style?

- Systems   To support what?

- Design   How define rewards?

                      Incentives?

- What measures are appropriate?

                      Can we measure performance?

                      Can people see this?

                      Is it manageable?

                      How is this communicated to everyone?

- Outcome   Effect on behaviour?

                      Success criteria?

- Monitoring   What review process do we have?

- We might also add costs

                      How much will it cost?

                      Is it worth it?

Performance management is usually taken to mean an increased emphasis on specifying what is wanted and rewarding those individuals who are able to deliver it satisfactorily. The normal stages of performance management as described in the literature and by those advocating performance management are:

- There are written and agreed job descriptions, and they are reviewed regularly.

- There are objectives for the work group, which have been cascaded down from the organisation's strategic objectives.

- There are individual objectives derived from the above, which are jointly devised by appraiser and appraisee. These objectives are result- rather than task-oriented, are tightly defined and include measures to be assessed. The objectives are designed to stretch the individual and offer potential development as well as meeting business needs.

- There is a development plan, devised by the manager and the individual, detailing development goals and activities designed to enable the individual to meet his or her objectives. These could be competency based. The emphasis here is on managerial support and coaching.

- Assessment of objectives with ongoing formal reviews is practised on a regular basis; it is designed to motivate the appraisee and concentrate on developmental issues.

- There is usually also an annual assessment which affects pay received, depending on the performance in achieving the objectives.

For many organisations this has led to three separate interviews with staff: the appraisal interview which looks at the past performance, the performance interview which looks at what is expected for the next period and the development interview which deals with training and development needs and future career prospects. For some these might actually be carried out one after the other on the same day, but the distinction between the three is felt useful to keep the idea of performance management clear. One of the major advantages of performance management is that managers are forced to give emphasis to formal and planned employee development. Another advantage is that it also enforces a clear role description and set of objectives agreed by managers and individuals. On the down side, there is potential conflict between the aim of improving performance – which requires openness and a developmental approach – and the link with pay. This conflict is sometimes resolved by separating the performance development and performance pay reviews and holding them at different times of the year.

> How many of the performance management techniques have I experienced? Would it have been appropriate to have used more? How would this sit with the desire for some people to be seen as autonomous professionals?

STRATEGY AND PLANNING

Before we get on to the specifics of performance management, in the next chapter, let us look briefly at some of the ways in which people in organisations arrive at the strategies and targets that are supposed to start the whole process off. There are shelves of books on strategy and planning from all possible points of view. An interesting and influential British one is Kay (1993). Perhaps the most commonly used technique is the simple form of a SWOT analysis. This is a useful device for analysing the situation and then making some decisions.

- *Strengths* – what are the positive attributes of the organisation, department or group in this situation? This might include people, traditions, technology and know-how, customer loyalty, resources, location and reputation.

- *Weaknesses* – what are the negative attributes of the organisation, department or group in this situation? It might include any of the above.

- *Opportunities* – these are usually changes in the environment of the organisation, such as changes in the market, legislation, transport, economy, other competitors' positions or technology. A successful organisation needs to have sensitivity to pick up on these.

- *Threats* – these can be any of the above – particularly if changes are ignored or not noticed.

When the SWOT analysis has been done, the outcomes can be broken down into suitable chunks and used to inform individual objectives for people. The device can be used in all sorts of circumstance for both large and small projects.

Should you do a SWOT analysis of your current project? Would it be useful in helping you sort out where the bottle-necks are in your schedule, and help you to prioritise your work?

PERFORMANCE-RELATED PAY

The way in which people are rewarded is central to the regulation of the employment relationship. Pay arrangements are also central to any changes, including cultural initiatives, because they are the most tangible expression of the working relationship between employer and employee. Managerial perceptions of appropriate payment systems have been subject to considerable change and fluctuation over time. The basic principles of paying either for time or performance (or both) are at the heart of any system. Payment for time is relatively straightforward, with set hourly or weekly rates. Paying for performance is altogether more complicated. The nature of the performance and whether it is achieved by an individual or a group can both be considered. Over time many organisations end up with some hybrid system that includes both of these factors, as well as all sorts of custom and practice. For example, we (Weightman, Blandamer and Torrington (1991)) found that people in the North Western Regional Health Authority were paid on 2,008 different levels of pay; 78 per cent of these pay points had 10 people or fewer being paid that amount. We also found wide ranges for such things as weekly hours, annual holidays, pay for being 'on call' and so on.

It is outside the scope of this book to discuss the advantages and disadvantages of different pay systems – for further information on them see Kessler (1995). However, it is worth noting that the current fashion of 'pay for performance' approaches to managing performance can really only work in an environment in which the staff are given enough discretion in their jobs to be able to affect their actual performance in a significant way. Otherwise they will become cynical about the whole initiative. It is also the case that for performance-related pay schemes to make a significant difference to performance they add about 10 per cent to the salary bill. This is because the performance element of the pay needs to be substantial, say 30 per cent, to be motivating otherwise it feels derisory and not worth working for. This is not always affordable or appropriate.

Despite all this talk of performance management the reality is that a line manager's responsibilities for pay are often merely the administrative ones of ensuring the paper work associated with hours, overtime and rotas worked is up to date and returned in time for the pay records to be updated before the pay date. Pay administration is a classic Herzberg hygiene factor; if it is OK no one bothers, but if there is an administrative error then people can be very upset. However, things are changing. For example, in 1996 Price Waterhouse offered its staff a cafeteria of benefits that it called Flex. A cafeteria of benefits is where the employer offers a range of benefits and individuals choose their own combination up to a certain cost – rather like choosing food in a cafeteria. In this scheme:

- 80 per cent of the reward figure had to be taken in cash

- plus a minimum of 20 days' holiday

- plus a choice from 19 benefits such as holidays, pensions, health insurance, accident insurance, childcare vouchers, retail vouchers, company cars and health club membership at a discount.

This had a tax and National Insurance contribution benefit for the company as well as the obvious benefit for the individual. Mercury Telecommunications also have a large scheme like this.

A line manager is responsible for engendering commitment from the staff. Rewarding them in other ways than through pay are within their powers. People work for a variety of reasons as we saw in Chapter 12. To gain commitment rewards can be such things as valuing the contribution, allowing autonomy, supporting people through personal crises and generally treating people as they should be treated. The personal credibility and leadership of a manager will probably enhance the value of these rewards in the eyes of the staff.

Answer the following about your organisation: what does the pay you receive tell you about the organisation you work in? Do the terms and conditions of the people who work in your section vary? What about the non-qualified staff? What about the difference between the conditions of the core and periphery staff? In what ways are you rewarded other than financially?

ETHICS OF MANAGING PERFORMANCE

What right does anyone have to manage another person's performance? Can those senior in the hierarchy be blamed for the poor performance of an individual at work? When there is a serious accident questions such as these become focused. For example, was it the captain of the ship who failed to close the doors who was responsible for the sinking of the ship, or was it his bosses who were constantly putting pressure on the captain to quicken the turn-around time in order to make more journeys per day? This discussion of the social responsibility and ethics of organisations is increasingly a subject for discussion – see for example Connock and Johns (1995).

We have earlier distinguished between hard and soft approaches to managing people. So it is with performance management. Those with a hard approach will see it as a continuing right and responsibility of those senior in the organisation to set out formal requirements for performance and to monitor the results. Those with a softer approach will prefer to see the developing individual as having the flair to cope with autonomy and consequently offering his or her best performance to the organisation.

These two approaches are at the extremes and most organisations use a mixture of both. Increasingly these are brought together in the contract of employment. This has explicit aspects that detail the ways in which the employer can control the work of the employee and what the employee will get in return. It also has implicit aspects, sometimes called the psychological contract, which include such things as that the employer will maintain mutual trust and confidence and that the employee will obey lawful and reasonable orders. This explicit and implicit contract of employment is at the core of performance management. See Foot and Hook (1996) for further discussion of this.

Some of these issues have been brought together under the concept of job satisfaction. Although originally studied from the point of view of motivation studies, job satisfaction seems to be something more complex than that and is now associated with job design and the quality of working life. Whatever is involved job satisfaction does seem to be an attitude of mind and is undoubtedly an internal state associated with a feeling of achievement. The relationship between job satisfaction and performance is controversial. Earlier researchers felt that satisfaction led to improved performance but it could be that performance leads to satisfaction. However, Luthans (1992, p123) suggests that:

> Although most people assume a positive relationship, the preponderance of research evidence indicates that there is no strong linkage between satisfaction and productivity.

The important concept to help make sense of performance management from an organisation perspective is that of some sort of contract between the employee and employer. The nature of the contract will vary enormously and individuals vary in what they consider acceptable. Analysing these contracts will tell you a good deal about the particular organisational behaviour.

DEFINING WHAT PERFORMANCE IS

Who defines what performance is required and whether it has been achieved will be determined by the nature of the organisation, its environment and the politics and power associated with the players involved. This context is dealt with in Chapters 7 and 11. Whoever runs the organisation ultimately is responsible for its performance. They may be accountable to shareholders, customers, clients, staff, the country and other stakeholders. The performance can be organisational, group or individual.

The interaction between members of the organisation over performance will be both formal and informal. We will often say to colleagues 'That's great' or 'What's that you're doing?' We will observe their behaviour, look at their production, listen to them on the telephone or see them with a client. These observations give us informal information about performance. We are constantly on the lookout for clues as to what others are doing and learning about their performance and picking up on what is acceptable and what is unacceptable performance in this particular context. We are also perhaps learning new ways to do things that improve our own performance. For example, my ability to use word processing was greatly improved by sitting next to an experienced secretary whilst we finished a report – she was wizard at using all the devices! Performance management involves formal, systematic ways of gaining information about performance.

The main construct of performance management is that work groups and individuals see what they have to do to make their contribution to the organisation's overall effectiveness. There needs to be a clear link with the organisational objectives. This involves good communication of clear objectives that everyone can understand. The level of involvement of individuals is contingent on the particular culture of the organisation. The organisation's strategy will be stated in various ways, from the formal written business plan to informal chats with senior staff. The performance is managed by the following processes:

- Organisation-wide

    incentives

    TQM

    quality assurance procedures such as BS5750 and ISO9000

    Investors in People

    learning organisation

- Team/department-wide

    team reviews

    performance indicators

    team incentives

    quality circles

    assessment

- Individual

    performance appraisal

    link to job description

    development plan

    performance-related pay.

These are discussed throughout the book; the next chapter in particular looks at individual performance management.

One approach to directing the performance of people in organisations is Management by Objectives (MBO). This phrase is used to describe a system of management that tries to relate the organisational goals to the behaviour and performance of individuals in the organisation. It involves:

- setting targets and objectives
- getting individuals to agree these objectives and the criteria for measuring performance
- continually appraising and reviewing the outcomes.

This concept was introduced by Drucker (1954) and was initially related to the behaviour of senior managers. Since then it has been widely adopted and is now applied to all levels in the organisation through performance-appraisal systems. The cycle of management by objectives is a cycle of interrelated activities see Figure 6.

Figure 6 **The MBO cycle**

The advantages claimed for such a system of performance management are that it:

- concentrates on the areas perceived to be important

- identifies problem areas before they become critical

- identifies training needs

- improves communications

- makes managers actually manage their staff.

Some difficulties, identified by Kane and Freeman (1986), are that:

- individuals do just enough to get the reward

- the emphasis is on the short term

- there is a lack of discretion for managers

- flexibility is lost as individuals 'work to objectives'

- there is an annual bottle-neck of interviews after the organisation's goals have been set.

An overriding issue for some is that it can be a top-down procedure if there is no feedback to the original target-setting from those asked to implement them. The next chapter deals with this in more detail.

AND FINALLY...

What would you recommend to Helena? Would you use any of the approaches in this chapter? Some sort of performance management? I would certainly recommend that Helena discuss this with the other seniors. I would also recommend that they as a firm set out their objectives and expectations clearly to the juniors. The nature of the 'mentoring' would also be an area to look at. Kate needs immediate attention, with suggestions on how her performance can be improved, and frequent appraisal-type discussions as follow up.

FURTHER READING

Current practice is often discussed in the management pages of the *Financial Times* and other broadsheet newspapers. Look at current personnel journals such as *People Management* from CIPD for specific examples of this practice. Any human resource management textbook will have material on this – for example, Foot and Hook (1996).

There are several videos in this area you might like to try:

- *The Whole Picture – 360-degree appraisal* – four case studies such as ICL and Thomas Cook from the Industrial Society (1997).

- *Coaching for Improved Performance at Work* – case studies such as NatWest and Easyjet from the Industrial Society (1997). These can be hired by the day.

- *Feedback for Performance* (1997) Melrose.

14 Performance management

OBJECTIVES

By the time you have finished reading this chapter you should be able to:

- understand and describe the basic ingredients for the effective design and operation of a performance review and appraisal system

- understand and describe systematic techniques for dealing with problems of poor performance.

MARGARET'S REVIEW

Margaret is the station manager for a medium-sized radio station. Recently it has been taken over by one of the larger media groups. She has been told that she should conduct a series of interviews with the staff who work for her at the station about their performance and development within the new context. She is deeply suspicious that this may be a precursor to redundancies. She has been assured that this is not so, but rather that the larger company has a policy of managing the performance of the staff systematically through a series of regular interviews. She receives a copy of their policy suggesting they have review interviews to discuss last year's performance, target-setting interviews to discuss next year's performance and development interviews to discuss individual development needs. Margaret has never heard anything like it. What is she to do?

Should she show the document to the staff? Discuss it with other members of management? Ask to go through the procedure herself with her boss first? Look for alternatives? See it as an opportunity to get to know her staff better? Just get on with it and not worry about the consequences? Have a joint training session with the staff on performance management and appraisal interviews? Say she does this informally anyway and sees no reason to put it in this grandiose procedure when everyone is very busy and having to work to new procedures after the take over?

'Managing performance' has become a buzz-phrase of management. What is meant by performance management or managing performance varies enormously. For some it means manipulating pay and other reward systems so that people will work harder. For others it means telling staff what they should do. Other people think it means increasing people's understanding of the whole process so that they know what they are doing. We will look at a variety of different models or methods in this chapter and some of the variety of claims that are made about managing performance.

The one certain thing is that nothing quite distinguishes our underlying assumptions about the working relationship as our approach to managing performance and what is seen as acceptable and what is not. Some would argue for the autonomy of individuals to offer their work in whatever way they feel is appropriate. Some would argue that there is a need for outside authorities to ensure standards that individuals apply in their work, although the individual is able to offer this work as and when he or she wishes (see, for example, professional groups such as lawyers and doctors). Others, usually managers, want things much more tightly controlled by the employers or managers. Questions about what, how, quality and rewards for work are all associated with performance management. Who should take the decisions about these are inevitably wrapped up in the politics of the debate.

This chapter looks at some of the issues associated with performance management as well as describing some of the normal sequence of procedures for managing performance.

Measuring anything about people inevitably means judging them in some way. Despite efforts to try to reduce the subjectiveness of this judgement, such as the use of a competency approach, there is always a point at which someone is judging another. Where this judgement is to last a long time and may affect the individual's chances of employment or education very careful consideration of the assessment process is necessary. This may explain why you can find almost mystical discussion of the assessment process in education journals. Table 16 gives a list of basic questions to ask about measuring someone's performance.

The answers to these questions will be contingent on the particular setting of the assessment.

Table 16 **Questions to ask yourself about measuring performance**

Why are we assessing this person?
- to recruit?
- to develop?
- to promote?
- to redeploy?
- to gain national qualifications?

How important is it that the assessment is very accurate?

Is the assessment compulsory?

How much time and effort are we prepared to put into the process?

How frequently do we want the assessment done?

Who should do the judging?
- the person him- or herself?
- his or her colleagues?
- someone in a position of authority?
- someone with expertise?
- a variety of people?

What sort of evidence is needed to assess the competency?
- can the individual collect written materials to prove that he or she has done something?
- must the competency be observed?
- are simulated exercises appropriate for assessing these competencies?
- can the competency be demonstrated in the course of normal work?

Who has sight of the conclusions of the assessment?
- is it confidential?
- just the individual, his or her line manager and personnel records?
- can the information be used for purposes other than the original?
- should the assessment result be used outside the unit?

What will happen as a result of the assessment?

Who is responsible for ensuring that any follow-up takes place?

PERFORMANCE APPRAISAL

Performance appraisal is a well-established way of providing milestones, feedback, guidance and monitoring for staff. A further development, as described above, is tying this appraisal into a larger and more complete system of performance management. These performance management systems, which are increasingly used (see for example Fletcher 1997), highlight appraisal as an activity central to the good management of staff. The difference from traditional appraisal 'chats' is that the assessment process in performance management tends to be more rigorous and objective, it is clearly linked to precise job definitions, it is based on organisational objective-setting and individual development plans and it has links with the pay system. For many systems an element of self-appraisal is also included, which has the advantage that it involves the individuals being assessed – who really know what they have been doing. They can suggest ways of improving their own work. Self-appraisal is also useful in engendering commitment to any agreed changes.

The essential elements of any performance appraisal are judgement and reporting. The performance is not simply being measured as in the completion of a work rota, it is being judged. This obviously involves discretion, worry about bias and the possibility of being quite wrong. This judgement not only has to be made but also passed on to other people in such a way that the other understands what is intended and takes action upon it. Those devising performance-appraisal schemes devote most of their energies to finding ways of making the judgements as systematic as possible and the reporting of different appraisers as consistent as possible.

Much of what has been written about the appraisal process concentrates on the personal interaction. In addition, George (1986) suggests that an effective appraisal scheme is dependent on the style and content of appraisal not conflicting with the culture of the organisation. He suggests that the degree of openness that is required in the appraisal process is 'unlikely to materialise without an atmosphere of mutual trust and respect – something which is conspicuously lacking in many employing organisations' (George 1986, p32). The appraisal, therefore, needs to reflect the wider values of the organisation in order for it to be properly integrated into the organisation and to survive in an effective form. The appraisal system can in fact be used to display and support the culture and style of the organisation.

The reasons why managers might want to appraise their staff include:

- human resource considerations – to ensure that the abilities and energies of individuals are being used effectively. They would hope to find out more about the staff and make better use of each individual's talents and expertise.

- training – it is useful to identify training needs both for new tasks and to improve poor performance amongst their staff.

- promotion – talking to individuals about their aspirations as well as finding out about their performance can assist decision-making about who is ready for promotion.

- planning – to identify skill shortages and succession needs. If there is a widespread lack of particular skills then some serious planning will need to take place.

- authority – the appraisal system sustains the hierarchy of authority by confirming the dependence of staff on those who manage them. It is one of the rituals which underline who is boss.

The reasons why staff might wish to be appraised by their managers include:

- performance – here is an opportunity to discuss what could be done and how one might go about doing it.

- motivation – talking about the job and the work it involves may remind us why we do the job and why we wanted it in the first place.

- career – bosses can be helpful as they understand the promotion route well, since they have travelled up it themselves.

Many things can impair the judgement, reporting and effectiveness of the performance appraisal. For example:

- prejudice

- insufficient knowledge of the individual

- the 'halo' effect of general likeability or recent events

- the difficulty of distinguishing the performance from the context in which the person works

- different perceptions of what are appropriate standards

- marking everyone 'just above average'

- ignoring the outcome of the appraisal process. For example, everyone will be frustrated if there are no improved resources, training or changes.

Despite these problems of judgement, reporting and follow-up, the potential advantages of performance appraisal are generally felt to be so great that it is worth expending the effort to make it work.

Most people find a problem-solving approach the most effective form of appraisal interview, as long as both appraiser and appraisee have the skill and ability to handle the situation. This approach is similar to the counselling interview where neither party knows the answer before the interview begins. It develops as the interaction takes place. Training in this type of interviewing is widely available. This does not mean that no preparation is required before the interview – indeed, quite the contrary. Both parties need to have a good think about the last year's performance, the next year's expectations and where the changes are expected. It is the comparison of each of their views of these that can be the real stuff of a trusting, problem-solving appraisal interview. Experience suggests that the quality of the interview improves as the confidence and trust of the participants develop. Do not expect too much the first time!

Here is a brief list of the stages in a counselling interview:

1 Factual interchange – focus on the facts of the situation first. Ask factual questions and provide factual information. This provides a basis for later analysis.

2 Opinion interchange – open the matter for discussion by asking the client's opinions and feelings but not offering any criticism or making any decisions. Gradually the matter is better understood by counsellor and client.

3 Joint problem solving – ask the client to analyse the situation described. The role of the counsellor is to assist in the analysis and focusing, not to produce answers.

4 Decision making – the counsellor helps to generate alternative lines of action for the client to consider and they both share in deciding what to do. Only the client can behave differently.

Performance appraisal in various guises is now very common. Different forms are constantly introduced to try to resolve some of the difficulties listed above. Despite the problems most people feel that a regular, formal encounter between themselves and their boss is an appropriate, if sometimes disappointing, procedure.

> Why do we appraise in our department? What is in it for the appraisee? What is in it for the appraiser?

Who should judge the performance and how should it be done?

Different types of assessment could include:

- self assessment – where individuals decide whether they are having difficulty or not with some required behaviour and this can then be the basis of discussion.

- peer assessment – not usually done formally unless in examining how effective the team is. But a great deal of informal measurement is done. Clergy in the Church of England are not considered employees because they 'work for God', so when they wanted to introduce appraisal they opted for peer appraisal.

- boss assessment – the most common technique in the work place. This may include observation, exercises and collecting evidence. Usually it does not involve such systematic measures and is much more informal.

- assessment by others who come into contact with the job-holder – for a true 360-degree picture of the job-holder some assessment by his or her customer/clients or other contacts would be logical, but rarely happens in works organisations. WH Smith use upward and 360-appraisal to identify manager's training and development needs.

- assessment by outsiders – this is sometimes used to give a certain objectivity, for example in assessment centres. It can be expensive and there is the question of confidentiality.

Techniques for assessing performance could include:

- observation – this can be both formal and informal. It has the advantage that the assessor actually sees the behaviour to be judged. It has high credibility, but it is very time-consuming. Not everything worth doing is observable.

- assessment or development centres – these are where individuals come together for a day or two and carry out various activities whilst being observed by assessors (see Woodruffe (1994)). They are useful for focusing on the individual and involving outsiders in the assessment. However, they are expensive to run and are simulations of activities rather than the real thing.

- portfolios – this is where individuals collect documents and evidence of work they have been involved in and done. The advantages are that individuals are responsible, the process celebrates achievement rather than failure and it concentrates on continuous development. However, portfolios can become very unwieldy to read through and there is the issue of comparability.

- record systems – such as work sheets. They enable comparisons with others but may emphasise quantity at the expense of quality.

> Whom do we involve? Should there be others? How do we do it?

Problems associated with performance-management schemes

The problems encountered in running any scheme of assessment are formidable. Here are a few of them, mostly based on the experience of appraisal schemes in organisations:

- Paperwork – any system of assessment always involves paperwork and documentation as the essential feature is reporting and schemes invariably include attempts to make the judgements and the reporting consistent between different assessors. This unavoidably involves forms and detailed instructions.

- Formality – the forms introduce an inhibiting feature into the everyday working relationships between the participants, who usually dislike the idea of formal evaluation. However, the desire for informality has to be balanced against the usefulness of a considered view.

- Outcomes ignored – often a development or promotion is agreed at the appraisal review and then the manager responsible does not deliver the promised development or promotion. There may be good reasons for this, but if it happens too often it can undermine the whole process.

- Performance measured by proxy – this is where the performance cannot be measured easily so some other behaviour, such as time-keeping or a pleasant manner, is measured instead. This is the 'halo' effect.

- Easily measured bits – people do the easily measured bits get the bonus whereas the difficult, soft parts of the job are ignored. This can become a powerful message in the organisation: everyone becomes more and more hard headed and wonders why they are all feeling so stressed.

- The just-above-average syndrome – there is a reluctance to say that people are not good enough, so many assessment schemes introduce a forced marking-down of some area so that not everything for everyone is marked just above average. Where this happens the high flyers continue to be developed and promoted but nothing is done to develop and deal with poor performance.

- Incomplete coverage – no system ever covers everyone. For example, those who have just arrived and those just leaving will not be covered. Where there are others being excluded because they are 'past it' or 'on the fast track' this can undermine the system.

- Ill-informed assessors – sometimes assessors are asked to carry out the assessment because of their job titles or rank rather than because of their knowledge of the job and the job holder's performance. The problem can be even worse if the assessors do not know the context in which the individual is trying to operate.

What problems do we have? Any of the above? What can do to improve?

POOR PERFORMANCE

A particular aspect of managing performance is managing the poor performer. We can all perform badly at times. Usually there is some tolerance of this but where it persists something has to be done about it for the sake of customers/clients, other colleagues and the individual concerned. Avoiding the issue of managing poor performance does not mean that it goes away. Problems with people at work can be short-term or long-term. For example, most of us are not very good when we have a cold; but there are others who never seem to perform well. It is these individuals who have a long-term performance problem that I want to discuss.

Before anything can be done to improve poor performance it is important to establish that there really is a gap between required and actual performance. Required performance can be communicated to individuals in several ways:

- contracts of employment with an outline of duties

- formal rule books

- job descriptions

- training manuals

- lists of standards

- procedures

- briefing meetings

- training sessions

- meetings

- individual conversations

- professional training and monitoring.

There may be reasons for an individual having difficulties with any of these. For example, the written requirements may be poorly thought out, inappropriate or out of date. Any of them may be poorly communicated.

When we need information about actual performance, this can be collected in several ways. For example:

- personal files

- time sheets

- sickness and absence records

- record cards

- customer complaints

- inaccurate work

- mistakes

- colleagues

- comparison with other people's work

- unfinished work.

After looking at what is expected and what has actually been done the question is whether there is sufficient gap between the two to require attention.

If a gap is established the next task is to find the reason for the gap. Only by finding the reason or reasons for the gap can we begin to do something about it. There are three main types of reason for poor performance. First are personal reasons that arise from the person's domestic and individual circumstances. These are outside the organisation's control. The main issue is how long and to what extent do we allow personal problems to interfere with work. Second are reasons to do with poor management and organisation. Third are individual reasons that arise from the individual not fitting in with the organisation. See Table 17.

Table 17 Reasons for problem performance

Personal characteristics
intellectual ability inappropriate due to poor selection or changes
lack of emotional stability due to poor selection or changes
poor physical ability which may change with age or job changes
health problems
domestic circumstances such as child care, parents or partner
family breakup.

Organisational characteristics
assignment and job impossible to do or understand
lack of suitable planning
job changes do not make sense to the individual
pay felt to be too low or poorly administered
poor investment in equipment
inadequate training
inappropriate levels of discipline – may be too excessive or too lenient
poor management – an individual poor manager or a poor management
    system
physical conditions distract from performance if they are irritating
location and transport problems when relocated.

Individual characteristics
group dynamics, where someone does not fit in and is excluded or
    prevented from fitting in
personality clash – this usually means one of the other reasons, but we
    all feel this clash occasionally
sense of fair play abused when different views on the right way to do or
    say things come into conflict
conflict of religious or moral values
inappropriate levels of confidence – may be over- or underconfident
poor motivation – although usually this really is a symptom of some
    other reason
poor understanding of the job despite everyone's effort.

Having established the gap in performance and found the reasons for it we are in a better position to do the main management work, which is to do something about it. Usually having established some of the reasons will give us starting points for dealing with them. There are some other starting points given in Table 18. Whatever the starting point there is a need to discuss the problem performance with the individual concerned; a counselling interview technique, based on problem solving such as the list above, would be appropriate.

Table 18 **Ways of dealing with the poor performer**

The following are not given in order of execution but as starting points to assist thinking when a problem arises.

- *Goal-setting.* Jointly agree specific, reasonable goals, and a date to review the performance.

- *Training.* Make sure you give appropriate training, preferably on the job, so there is no problem in making the connection between the training and the working situation.

- *Dissatisfactions.* Fill the gap where appropriate; remedy particular problems such as pay or conditions.

- *Discipline.* These range from the informal discussion through to increasingly formal procedures and punishment – ultimately including dismissal.

- *Reorganising.* This is appropriate where the problem has arisen through difficulties with the work materials, reporting relationships or physical arrangements no longer being adequately organised.

- *Management.* Improve the clarity of communicating the task, monitoring systems or the expertise of a particular manager.

- *Outside agencies.* These are particularly appropriate where there are personal and family reasons.

- *The job.* Transfer the individual to a more appropriate job or department; redesign the job.

- *Peer pressure.* Where an individual performance is very different from the average, those working alongside will feel it inappropriate and may put pressure on the individual to change.

DISCIPLINE AND DISMISSAL

All the previous sections have been about disciplining, in the sense of trying to change someone's performance, but at some point a manager may feel that the process needs to be more formal. It is, however, advisable to keep records of what has happened from the earliest stages just in case things reach the point of formal procedures.

Most organisations will have procedures for discipline and dismissal. The personnel department and Trade Union representatives will know them in detail. It is worth consulting them to ensure that you follow the procedures. Many employers use the ACAS code of practice (1977) as the basis of their procedures. ACAS has also published an advisory booklet *Discipline at Work* (1987), which is strongly recommended – see Table 19 for a summary. There are several areas that may lead to disciplinary procedures besides poor performance – for example, where rules necessary to maintain standards have been broken such as those covering absence, health and safety, misconduct, the use of company facilities, timekeeping and holiday arrangements.

When all the above ideas, and no doubt others as well, have been tried but have failed to improve performance, there comes a point when a decision to dismiss the problem person has to be faced. Where this is a possible outcome, it is important that procedure is closely adhered to. The legislation is clear. You are advised not to dismiss an employee without involving personnel or some other manager.

This chapter about performance management inevitably has a more managerial feel to it than some of the others. After all it has management in the title! Questions can be asked of one's right to manage someone else's performance – and when and how one does it. The contract of employment and how this is interpreted is at the heart of this relationship. Understanding performance management and some of the associated issues is important for analysing managing people.

Table 19 Checklist for handling a disciplinary matter

1 Gather all the relevant facts: promptly, before memories fade, take statements, collect documents, in serious cases consider suspension with pay while an investigation is conducted.

2 Be clear about the complaint: is action needed at this stage?

3 If so, decide whether the action should be:
- advice and counselling
- formal disciplinary action.

4 If formal action is required, arrange a disciplinary interview:
- ensure that the individual is aware of the nature of the complaint and that the interview is a disciplinary one
- tell the individual where and when the interview will take place and of a right to be accompanied
- try to arrange for a second member of management to be present.

5 Start by introducing:
- those present and the purpose of the interview
- the nature of the complaint
- the supporting evidence

6 Allow the individual to state his or her case:
- consider and question any explanations put forward.

7 If any new facts emerge:
- decide whether further investigation is required
- if it is, adjourn the interview and reconvene when the investigation is complete.

8 Except in very straightforward cases, call an adjournment before reaching a decision:
- come to a clear view about the facts
- if they are disputed, decide on the balance of probability what version of the facts is true.

9 Before deciding the penalty consider:
- the gravity of the offence and whether the procedure gives guidance
- the penalty applied in similar cases in the past
- the individual's disciplinary record and general service
- any mitigating circumstances
- whether the proposed penalty is reasonable in all the circumstances.

10 Reconvene the disciplinary interview to:
- clearly inform the individual of the decision and the penalty, if any
- explain the right of appeal and how it operates
- in the case of a warning, explain what improvement is expected, how long the warning will last and what the consequences of failure to improve may be.

11 Record the action taken:
- if other than an oral warning, confirm the disciplinary action to the individual in writing
- keep a simple record of the action taken for future reference.

12 Monitor the individual's performance:
- disciplinary action should be followed up, with the object of encouraging improvement
- monitor progress regularly and discuss it with the individual.

Source: ACAS, *Discipline at work*, London, ACAS, 1987.

AND FINALLY...

What would you do in Margaret's position? Is there anything of use in this chapter? If I were advising Margaret, I would suggest having a general one-hour meeting with the staff to discuss the document and to discuss what is meant by the performance interviews and also what is not meant by them. Who sees the final assessment documents and what they can be used for is an area of concern to many. This needs clarifying: are they to be used only within the department, or will they be used for promotion and redundancy purposes as well? I would suggest she starts in a small way using a problem-solving approach to one or two easily agreed targets.

References

REFERENCES

ACAS (1977) *Code of Practice: Disciplinary practice and procedures in employment*. Available from ACAS, London.

ACAS (1987) *Discipline at Work*. London, ACAS.

ACAS (1994) *Recruitment and Induction*. London, ACAS.

ADAIR J (1982) *Action-Centred Leadership*. Aldershot, Gower.

ADAMS JS (1979) 'Injustice in social exchange' in Steers and Porter, *Motivation and Work Behaviour*. 2nd edn. Maidenhead, McGraw-Hill.

ALDERFER CP (1972) *Existence, Relatedness and Growth*. New York, Free Press.

ALLPORT FH (1954) 'The structuring of events: outline of a general theory with applications to psychology'. *Psychological Review*. 61. pp281–303.

ARGYRIS C and SCHON D (1978) *Organizational Learning: A theory in action perspective*. New York, Addison-Wesley.

ARMSTRONG M (1996) *Employee Reward*. London, Institute of Personnel and Development.

BANDURA A (1977) *Social Learning Theory*. Hemel Hempstead, Prentice Hall.

BEE F and BEE R (1994) *Training Needs Analysis and Evaluation*. London, Institute of Personnel and Development.

BEYNON H (1973) *Working for Ford*. Harmondsworth, Penguin Books.

BLAUNER R (1967). *Alienation and Freedom: The factory worker and his industry*. Chicago, University of Chicago Press.

BLAKE RR *and* MOUTON JS (1969) *Building a Dynamic Organization through Grid Organization Development*. Houston, Texas, Gull.

BOWDEN V (1997) 'The career states system model: a new approach to analysing careers'. *British Journal of Guidance and Counselling*. Vol 25. No 4. pp 473–490.

BRAMHAM J (1989) *Human Resource Planning*. London, Institute of Personnel Management.

BRYANS P P *and* CRONIN TP (1983) *Organization Theory*. London, Mitchell Beazley.

BURNS JM (1978) *Leadership*. New York, Harper and Row.

BURREL G *and* MORGAN G (1979) *Sociological Paradigms and Organisational Analysis*. London, Heinemann.

CARTER A (1979) *Authority and Democracy*. London, Routledge and Kegan Paul.

CONNOCK S *and* JOHNS T (1995) *Ethical Leadership*. London, Institute of Personnel and Development.

COOPER C *and* EARNSHAW J (1996) *Stress and Employer Liability*. London, Institute of Personnel and Development.

DAHL R (1970) *Modern Political Analysis*. 2nd edn. Englewood Ciffs, New Jersey, Prentice-Hall.

DAVIES K (1972) *Human Behaviour at Work*. 4th edn. New York, McGraw-Hill.

DICKSON NS (1976) *The Psychology of Military Incompetence*. London, Jonathan Cape.

DRUCKER PF (1989) *The Practice of Management*. London, Heinemann Professional. (This includes reference to his earlier 1954 work.)

ETZIONI A (1975) *A Comparative Analysis of Complex Organizations: On power, involvement and their correlates*. Revised edn. New York, Free Press.

EYSENCK HJ (1962) *Know Your Own IQ*. Harmondsworth, Penguin.

EYSENCK H J (1976) *The Measurement of Personality*. Lancaster, MTP Press.

FARNHAM D (1999) *Managing in a Business Context*. London, Institute of Personnel and Development.

FIEDLER FE (1967) *A Theory of Leadership Effectiveness*. New York, McGraw-Hill.

FLETCHER C (1997) *Appraisal: Routes to improved performance*. 2nd edn. London, Institute of Personnel and Development.

FOOT M *and* HOOK C (1996) *Introducing Human Resource Management*. Harlow, Addison Wesley Longman.

FOY N (1994) *Empowering People at Work*. Aldershot, Gower.

FRASER MUNRO J (1950) *Employment Interviewing*. London, Macdonald and Evans.

FRENCH J *and* RAVEN B (1958) 'The Bases of Social Power' in CARTWRIGHT D ed., *Studies in Social Power*. Institute of Social Research. Michigan, Ann Arbor.

FREUD S (1962) *Two Short Accounts of Psychoanalysis*. Harmondsworth, Penguin Books.

GAGNE RM (1975) *Essentials of Learning for Instruction*. New York, Holt Reinehart and Winston.

GATES B (1996) *The Road Ahead*. Harmondsworth, Penguin.

GEORGE J (1986) 'Appraisal in the public sector: dispensing with the big stick'. *Personnel Management*. May. pp32–35.

GOLDTHORPE JH, LOCKWOOD D, BECHHOFER F *and* PLATT J (1969) *The Affluent Worker in the Class Struggle*. Cambridge, Cambridge University Press

GREENFIELD A (1997) *The Human Brain*. London, Weidenfeld and Nicolson.

GUERIN D (1970) 'Anarchism: from theory to practice'. *Monthly Review Press*.

HACKMAN JR (1987) 'Work design', in STEERS RM *and* PORTER LM eds, 4th edn. *Motivation and Work Behaviour*. London, McGraw-Hill.

HAMBLIN A (1974) *Evaluation and Control of Training*. London, McGraw-Hill.

HANDY C (1989) *The Age of Unreason*. London, Business Books.

HANDY C (1985) *Understanding Organisations*. Harmondsworth, Penguin.

HARVEY-JONES J (1994) *All together now*. London, Heinemann.

HENDRY C, BRADLEY P AND PERKINS S (1997) 'Missed a motivator?' *People Management*. 15 May 1997. pp20–25.

HERIOT P *and* PEMBERTON C (1995) *New Deals*. Chichester, Wiley.

HERRIOT P (1989) *Assessment and Selection in Organisations*. Chichester, Wiley.

HERZBERG F (1968) 'One more time: how do you motivate employees?' *Harvard Business Review*. Jan/Feb.

HONEY P *and* MUMFORD A (1992) *A Manual of Learning Styles*. 3rd edn. Honey, 10 Linden Avenue, Maidenhead.

HYMAN J *and* CUNNINGHAM I (1996) 'Empowerment in Organisations; Changes in the manager's role' in MEGGINSON D *and* GIBB S eds, *Managers as Developers*. Hemel Hempstead, Prentice-Hall.

ILES PA *and* SALAMAN G (1995) 'Recruitment, selection and assessment' in STOREY J ed., *Human Resource Management: A critical text*. London, Routledge.

INDUSTRIAL TRAINING UNIT RESEARCH UNIT (1976) *Choose an Effective Style: A self-instructional approach to the teaching of skills*. Cambridge ITRU based on E and RM Belbin, 1972, *Problems in Adult Retraining*. London, Heinemann.

IPD (1998) *Managing Diversity: An IPD position paper*. London, Institute of Personnel and Development.

JENKINS R (1986) *Racism and Recruitment: Managers, organizations and equal opportunities in the labour market.* Cambridge, Cambridge University Press.

KANDOLA R *and* FULLERTON J (1998) *Diversity in Action.* 2nd ed. London, Institute of Personnel and Development.

KANE JS *and* FREEMAN KA (1986) 'MBO and performance appraisal: a mixture that's not a solution'. *Personnel.* Vol. 63, No 12, Dec. pp26–36.

KANTER RM (1989) *When Giants Learn to Dance.* London, Simon and Schuster.

KATZ D *and* KAHN R L (1978) *The Social Psychology of Organizations.* 2nd ed. New York, Wiley.

KAY J (1993) *Foundations of Corporate Success: How Business strategies add value.* Oxford, Oxford University Press.

KELLY G (1955) *The Psychology of Personal Constructs.* New York, Norton.

KESSLER I (1995) *Reward Systems in Human Resource Management: A critical text.* J Storey ed. London, Routledge.

KLINE P (1989) *Psychology Exposed.* London, Routledge.

KOLB DA, RUBIN IM *and* McINTYRE (1974) *Organizational Psychology: An experimental approach.* London, Prentice-Hall.

KOLB DA, RUBIN IM *and* OSLAND J (1991) *Organizational Behaviour: An experiential approach.* 5th edn. London, Prentice-Hall.

KOTTER J (1982) *The General Managers.* New York, Free Press.

KRECH D, CRUTCHFIELD RS *and* BALLACHEY EL (1962) *Individual in Society.* New York, McGraw-Hill.

KRECH D *and* CLUTCHFIELD R (1948) *Theory and Problems of Social Psychology.* New York, McGraw-Hill.

KUHNERT KW *and* LEWIS P (1987) 'Transactional and transformational leadership: a constructive/developmental analysis'. *Academy of Management Review.* Oct. 1987. pp 648–57.

LEIGH T *and* BROWN S (1996) *Journal of Applied Psychology.* Aug.

LEWIN K (1952) *Field Theory in Social Science.* London, Tavistock Publications.

LOWNDS S (1998) *Fast Track to Change on the Heathrow Express.* London, Institute of Personnel and Development.

LUTHANS F (1992) *Organizational Behaviour.* 6th edn. Maidenhead, McGraw-Hill.

LUTHANS F *and* KREITNER R (1975) *Organizational Behaviour Modification.* Glenville Ill., Scott Foreman.

MCCALMAN J *and* PATON RA (1992) *Change Management: A guide to effective implementation.* London, Paul Chapman.

MARCHINGTON M *and* WILKINSON A (1996) *Core Personnel and Development.* London, Institute of Personnel and Development.

MARQUAND M *and* REYNOLDS A (1994) *The Global Learning Organisation.* London, Irwin.

MASLOW AH (1954) *Motivation and Personality.* New York, Harper and Row.

Mayo – the Hawthorne research is classically described in Roethlisberger FJ and Dickson WJ (1939) *Management and the worker.* Cambridge, Massachusetts, Harvard University Press.

MESTEL R (1994) 'Let the mind talk'. *New Scientist.* 23 July. pp26–31

MILLS CW (1956) *White Collar: The American middle classes.* New York, OUP.

MINTZBERG H (1973) *The Nature of Managerial Work.* London, Harper and Row.

MORGAN G (1986) *Images of Organization.* Newbury Park, Sage.

MORGAN G (1997) *Images of Organization.* 2nd ed. Beverly Hills, California, Sage Publications.

MULLINS LJ (1996) *Management and Organisational Behaviour.* London, Pitman.

MUMFORD E. (1972) 'Job satisfaction: a method of analysis' *Personnel Review*. Summer 1972.

PAVLOV I (1927) *Conditioned Reflexes*. Oxford, Oxford University Press

PEDLAR M, BURGOYNE J *and* BOYDELL T. (1991) *The Learning Company: A strategy for sustained development*. London, McGraw-Hill.

PETERS TJ *and* WATERMAN RH (1982) *In Search of Excellence*. New York, Harper and Row.

PFEFFER J (1981) *Power in Organizations*. Marshfield, Massachussetts, Pitman.

PRAHALAD CK *and* HAMEL G (1990) 'The core competence of the corporation'. *Harvard Business Review*. May/June. pp79–91.

PUGH DS (1971) *Organisational Theory*. London, Penguin.

REID MA *and* BARRINGTON H (1999) *Training Interventions*. 6th edn. London, Institute of Personnel and Development.

RICK S (1996) 'Managers as Developers or Developers as Managers?', in *Managers as Developers*. MEGGINSON D *and* GIBB S eds. Hemel Hempstead, Prentice-Hall.

RODGER A (1952) *The Seven-Point Plan*. London, National Institute of Industrial Psychology.

ROGERS C (1967) *On Becoming a Person*. London, Constable.

ROTHWELL S (1995) 'Human resource planning', in STOREY J ed., *Human Resource Management: A critical text*. London, Routledge.

ROWE D (1997) *The real meaning of money*. London, HarperCollins.

SCASE R *and* GOFFEE R (1989) *Reluctant Managers*. London, Unwin Hyman.

SCHEIN E (1978) *Career Dynamics: Matching individual and organisational needs*. Reading, Mass. Addison Wesley.

SKINNER BF (1953) *Science and Human Behaviour*. New York, Macmillan Free Press.

SKINNER BF (1965) *Science and Human Behaviour*. New York, Free Press.

STEERS RM *and* PORTER LW eds. (1987) *Motivation and Work Behaviour*. 4th edn. London, McGraw-Hill .

STEERS RM *and* PORTER LW eds. (1991) *Motivation and Work Behaviour*. 5th edn. London, McGraw-Hill .

STEWART R (1967) *Managers and their jobs*. London, Macmillan.

TANNENBAUM R *and* SCHMIDT WH (1973) 'How to choose a leadership pattern'. *Harvard Business Review*. May–June. pp162–75, 178–180.

TOFFLER A (1970) *Future Shock*. London, Pan Books.

TORRINGTON D *and* WEIGHTMAN J (1987) 'The analysis of management work'. *Training and Management Development methods*. pp27–33.

TORRINGTON DP *and* WEIGHTMAN JB (1989) *Effective Management*. 2nd edn. Hemel Hempstead, Prentice-Hall.

TORRINGTON DP *and* WEIGHTMAN JB (1989) *The Reality of School Management*. Oxford, Blackwell.

TORRINGTON D *and* WEIGHTMAN J (1982) 'Technical Atrophy in Middle Management'. *Journal of General Management*. pp5–17.

TYSON S (1987) 'The management of the personnel function'. *Journal of Management Studies*. pp523–32.

VROOM V AND DECI E (1974) *Management and Motivation*. London, Penguin Books.

WATSON CM (1983) 'Leadership, management and the seven keys'. *Business Horizons*. March–April. pp8–13.

WEIGHTMAN J *and* FLUDE R (1996) Report for Kelloggs. Unpublished.

WEIGHTMAN J (1993) *Managing Human Resources*. London, Institute of Personnel Management.

WEIGHTMAN J (1986) *'Middle Management: Dinosaur or dynamo?'* PhD thesis. Manchester, UMIST.

WEIGHTMAN J, BLANDAMER W *and* TORRINGTON D (1991) *Pay Structures and Negotiating Arrangements: Report for the North Western Regional Health Authority.*

WOLFF RP (1970) *In Defence of Anarchism.* London, Harper and Row.

WOODRUFFE C (1994) Assessment Centres. 2nd edn. London, Institute of Personnel and Development.

Professional standards index

This index cross-references to chapters in the text the main subject areas as set out in the Professional Standards of the Chartered Institute of Personnel and Development for *Managing People*:

INDICATIVE CONTENT

- Individual differences   2
- Attitudes and behaviour   2
- Learning   3, 13
- Psychological contract   4, 14
- People competencies   5, 10, 11
- New work patterns   5
- Stress   6
- Drive for leadership   7, 8, 9
- Commitment through leadership   10, 11
- Performance through motivation   12, 13, 14

Index

absolute values, ethics 13
accountability 160
acting up 129–30
action learning 130
Adair, J. 144, 145
added-value workers 62
agendas, and networking 161–2
Alderfer, C.P. 174
alienation 180–82
Allport, F.H. 31
application forms 118
architects, personnel departments
    compared to 8
assessment centres 119, 204
assessment of performance 198–9
attitudes 31–3, 45
    to work 179–80
attribution 23
audio-visual presentations 130
authority 156–60, 201
    see also power
autonomous work teams 68

behaviour
    modification 21, 37–8
    study of 4–5, 6
behaviourism 20–21, 37–8
Blake, R.R. 145
Blauner, R. 181
Boydell, T. 49
Bradley, P. 185
Bramham, J. 75
Brent Spar oil platform 59
British Airways 71
Brown, S. 175
Bryans, P.P. 101
Burgoyne, J. 49
Burns, J.M. 151

cafeteria benefits 190
career anchors 89
career development 138–9
caring responsibilities 29
Carter, A. 156
case-studies, training methods 130–31
change 85–90
    of attitudes 32–3, 45
    innovation overload 108
    and learning 35–6
    management of 87–90
    technological innovation and 56–8
    types of 86
classical conditioning 37
clerks of works, personnel departments
    compared to 8
coaching 131
commitment, and compliance 97–110
competencies 10
    and job design 70
    leadership 142, 151–2
    managerial 11–12
    and recruitment processes 114
    and training needs analysis 127–8
comprehension 44
conditioning
    classical 37
    operant 37
conflict 100–02
consideration 109
consultation 109–10
consumer expectations 59
contingency models of leadership
    147–9
contingency theory 9
continuous professional development
    (CPD) 138
contract staff 77–9

contracts managers, personnel
  departments compared to 8
contracts of employment 122
control 98–9, 102–3
  see also power
Control of Substances Hazardous to
  Health Regulations (COSHH) 93
core staff 71, 77, 78, 79, 115–16, 170
counselling 91–2
CRAMP taxonomy of learning 44–6
credibility 157–9
Cronin, T.P. 101
Crutchfield, R.S. 32, 143
culturally determined motivations 169
Cunningham, I. 107
curricula vitae (CVs) 119
customer expectations 58–9

Dahl, R.A. 99
Davies, K. 142
Deci, E. 176
defence mechanisms 18
delegation 109, 131, 159–60
  see also empowerment
departmental organisation 65, 69–70
development *see* training and
  development
disability 29
discipline 210, 211
discrimination 26–7, 121–2
discussion, training methods 132
dismissal 210
distance learning 132
diversity 26–30
dysfunctional expectancies 23–4
dysfunctional self-evaluation 24

economic conditions, influence on
  employment market 55, 59–60
ego, psychoanalytical theory 17
employability 61–2, 138
employment environment 54–8
employment law *see* legislation
empowerment 106–8
  see also delegation
environment, of the employment
  relationship 54–8
environmental practice 59
equal opportunities 26–7
  see also discrimination
esteem needs 171, 172, 173

ethics
  of behaviour modification 21
  of leadership 13–14
  of performance management 191
ethnic minorities 29
Etzioni, A. 102–3
evaluation of training 136–7
exchange theory 177
exercises, training methods 132
expectancy theory 176–7
experience 36
experiential learning 40–41
experimental psychology, and learning
  theory 38–9
experimentation, learning processes
  40
extroverted personalities 19
Eysenck, Hans 19–20

feedback 39, 109
Fiedler, F.E. 147–9
five-fold grading system 114, 115
flexibility 71–2
  see also periphery staff
flexible benefits 190
flexible working hours 71–2
Flude, Royston 11, 12
force-field theory 176
Fraser, J. Munro 114, 115
Freeman, K.A. 195
French, J. 103–4
Freud, Sigmund 17–19

Gagne, R.M. 38
gender composition of workforce 29
generalisation, learning processes 39,
  40
George, J. 200
globalisation 55–6
Goldthorpe, J.H. 179
group dynamics 132
Guerin, D. 156

Hackman, J.R. 66, 67
'halo effect' 30, 202, 205
Hamblin, A. 137
hard management 10, 11–12, 191
Hawthorne experiments 6, 124
health and safety 93–4
Heathrow Express Construction
  Project 152

Hendry, C. 185
Herriot, P. 61
Herzberg's theory of motivation 174–5
hierarchy of needs (Maslow) 22,
    170–74
Honey, P. 43
hot-desking 57–8
human resource management 7–8
human resource planning 74–7
humanistic psychology 21–3
hygiene factors, motivation 174, 175
Hyman, J. 107

id, psychoanalytical theory 17
Images of Organisation (Morgan) 2
induction 123
influence 154–67
innovation 56–8, 108
    see also change
interviews
    counselling 92, 202–3
    disciplinary 211
    performance management 187,
        202–3
    selection 119–20
introverted personalities 19
Investors in People 138
involvement 102–3
    see also participation

job analysis 114
job descriptions 113–14
job design 65–72
job enlargement 66, 68
job enrichment 68
job rotation 66, 133
job satisfaction 66–8, 179–82, 191–2
job security 60, 61–2

Kahn, R.L. 32
Kane, J.S. 195
Kanter, R.M. 61–2
Katz, D. 32
Kelly, G. 23
Kolb, D.A.
    learning cycle 40–41
    learning styles 41–3
Kotter, J. 149, 160
Krech, D. 32, 143
Kuhnert, K.W. 151

leadership 140–53
    competencies 142, 151–2
    contingency models of 147–9
    continuum of control 98–9, 108
    credibility 157–9
    definition of 141
    distinguished from management
        9–12, 149–50
    ethics of 13–14
    and job satisfaction 68
    roles 143–4
    styles 144–9
    traits related to success 141–2
    transactional and transformational
        151
learning 35–51
    behaviourist theory 20–21, 37–8
    and change 35–6
    CRAMP taxonomy of 44–6
    cycles 40–41
    experiential learning 40–41
    experimental psychology findings
        38–9
    individual differences in 41–3
    opportunities for 133
    role theory 46–7
    social learning theories 23–4
    styles 41–3
learning contracts 133
learning organisations 48–50, 138
lectures 133–4
legislation
    employment environment 54–5
    equal opportunities 26–7, 121–2
    health and safety 93–4
legitimacy of authority 158
Leigh, T. 175
Lewin, K. 176
Lewis, P. 151
lifelong learning 137–8
Lilly Industries 72
listening, counselling skills 91
Luthans, F. 192

management
    distinguished from leadership
        9–12, 149–50
    hard management 10, 11–12, 191
    soft management 10–12, 191
    trends in 81–2

Management by Objectives (MBO) 194–5
managerial competencies 11–12
managerial grid (Blake and Mouton) 145–6
managing diversity see diversity
Marquand, M. 48
Maslow's model of motivation 22, 170–4
meetings 163–6
memory 38–9, 45
mentoring 92–3
Mills, C.W. 170
morale 108–10
Morgan, Gareth 2
motivation 168–83
   and attitudes 32, 179–80
   expectancy theory 176–7
   force-field theory 176
   Herzberg's theory 174–5
   and learning 38
   Maslow's model 170–74
   and work behaviour 177–82
Mouton, J.S. 145
Mullins, L.J. 159
Mumford, A. 43

needs, Maslow's hierarchy of 22, 170–74
negotiation 162–3
networking 160–62
neuroticism 19
new technologies see technological innovation

objectives 186–7
   see also Management by Objectives (MBO)
observation, assessment techniques 204
Occupational Personality Questionnaire (OPQ) 24
offers of employment 122
on-the-job training 134
operant conditioning 37
OPQ 24
organisation of operational units 65, 68–70
organisational politics 99–106
organisational psychology 5
organisations 2–3, 8–9, 100
orientation to work 179–80

participation 98–9, 109–10
   see also involvement
Pavlov, Ivan 37
pay 189–90
Pedlar, M. 49
peer assessment 203
Pemberton, C. 61
perception 24–6, 38
performance
   appraisal 200–06
   management 184–210
   measurement 198–9
   problems 206–9
performance-related pay 185, 189–90
periphery staff 71, 77–9, 170
Perkins, S. 185
person specifications 114, 115
personal construct theory 23
personal development 137–9
personality, theories of 16–24
personnel departments, compared to architects 8
personnel management 7–8
persuasion 154–67
PEST framework 54
Pfeffer, J. 100
planning 73–7
pluralist view of organisations 8–9, 100–01
politics
   influence on employment environment 54–5
   within organisations 99–106, 161
poor performance 206–9
Porter, L.W. 173, 178
portfolios, assessment techniques 204
power 99–100
   in employment relationship 60
   individual sources of 103–6
   within organisations 102–3
   see also authority; control
prejudice 30–31
presentations 166, 167
procedural learning 45
programmed instruction 134
programmed learning 20, 37
projects, training methods 134
promotion 201
psychoanalytical theory 17–20
psychological contract 60–3, 169–70, 191
psychology 4–5, 6

learning theory 36–43
perception 24–6
theories of personality 16–24
psychometric tests 24, 120

quality movement 10, 68
quality standards 10, 58–9

Raven, B. 103–4
recall 39
recruitment agencies 120
recruitment methods 116–22
references 120
reflex learning 44–5
reinforcement, and learning 20–21, 37
repertory grid 23
responsibility 159–60
retention, learning processes 38–9
reward 177–8
behaviourist theory 20–21, 37
pay 189–90
Reynolds, A. 48
Rodger, A. 114, 115
Rogers, Carl 22
role-play 135
role theory 46–7
Royal Bank of Scotland 81–2

S-R learning 37
satisfiers, motivation 174, 175
Schein, E. 89
Schmidt, W.H. 98
Scottish Office 57–8
secondments 135
selection processes 118–22
self-actualisation 22, 171, 173, 180
self-assessment 200, 203
self-development 137–9
seven-point plan 114, 115
7-Ss 149
sex discrimination 27, 121–2
simulations 135
skill instruction 136
skill shortages 56
Skinner, B.F. 20, 37
social learning theories 23–4, 46–7
social needs 171, 172, 173
social sciences 2, 4–6
socialisation 26, 47
of new employees 123–4
sociological perspective on learning
46–7

sociology 5–6
soft management 10–12, 191
stability zones 88–9
staffing
human resource planning 74–7
reduction of costs 73
Steers, R.M. 173, 178
stereotyping 30–31
stress 80–95
application of humanistic
psychology 22
causes of 83–4
change and 85–90
counselling 91–2
managing time 90–91
responses to 84–5
symptoms of 83
structures 65, 68–70
superego, psychoanalytical theory 17
SWOT analysis 188

talks, training methods 136
Tannenbaum, R. 98
task analysis 44
teams 141
technological innovation 56–8
temporary staff 77–9
tests 24, 120
time management 90–91
Toffler, A. 88
training and development 126–39
continuous development 137–9
development plans 187
evaluation of 136–7
identification of needs 127–8
methods 129–36
transactional leaders 151
transformational leaders 151
Tyson, S. 8

unitarist view of organisations 8–9,
100

vacancies, identification and
description of 112–16
valency, motivation theory 176
validation of training 136–7
values, ethics of leadership 13
valuing staff 108–10
Vauxhall Motor Company 179
Vroom, V. 176

Watson, C.M. 149
Wolff, R.P. 156
word-of-mouth recruitment 117
workplace design, effect of new
    technology 57–8

zero-hours contracts 72

The People and Organisations series and Core Management studies

The only route to a professional career in personnel and development is through the achievement of the CIPD's professional standards. One of the three fields that make up these standards, the new Core Management standards define the essentials for competently managing and developing people. They are compatible with an N/SVQ at Level 4 in management.

CIPD Publications has five books in the *People and Organisations* series as textbooks for the new Core Management standards. The texts of these five books and their titles closely follow the Core Management syllabus. The titles of the books are:

Managing Activities	Michael Armstrong
Managing Financial Information	David Davies
Managing in a Business Context	David Farnham
Managing People	Jane Weightman
Managing Information and Statistics	Roland and Frances Bee

Managing Financial Information
David Davies

Managing Financial Information is a practical explanation of the interface between the finance and HR functions in organisations. It analyses thoroughly many areas that managers may find daunting, and includes test questions and work-based exercises to assist competent learning.

It examines:

- balance sheets

- trading and profit and loss accounts

- budgeting

- costing.

David Davies is a principal lecturer in financial management at the University of Portsmouth. A qualified accountant with a Masters degree in management from Henley Management College, he previously spent 17 years in the private and public sectors. He currently lectures on post- and undergraduate courses, as well as undertaking consultancy work.

1999
£14.99
0 85292 782 7
Paperback
192 pages
246 x 177mm format

Managing in a Business Context

David Farnham

Managing in a Business Context illustrates the framework in which businesses are working in Britain today. Beginning with the nature of strategy and how strategy can be converted into practice, it then considers the issues of wider concern to HR practitioners and business managers in general.

It examines:

- economics, politics and political systems, and their effect on the workplace

- social and legal structures, and how they impinge on the private and public sectors

- the technological revolution and its effect on working practices

- business ethics and the impact of an international climate.

Professor David Farnham holds the chair in Employment Relations at the University of Portsmouth. He has also written *Employee Relations in Context*, published by the CIPD.

1999
£16.99
0 85292 783 5
Paperback
368 pages
246 x 177mm format

Managing Information and Statistics

Roland and Frances Bee

Managing Information and Statistics is a hands-on guide that explains how the apparently esoteric discipline of statistics can be an invaluable management tool. Tables, diagrams and graphs are explained in detail; surveys, forecasting and the principles of relationships between data each have their own sections.

It examines:

- how to produce reports and presentations to the highest standard

- how to use general statistical packages

- how to apply statistical thinking to people-management issues

- how to manage data effectively.

Frances and Roland Bee are experienced training consultants and have written three other highly successful CIPD books – *Training Needs Analysis and Evaluation*, *Constructive Feedback*, *Customer Care* and *Project Management*.

1999
£15.99
0 85292 785 1
Paperback
336 pages
246 x 177mm format